The Rep Coach

Fayaz Shah

authorHOUSE®

AuthorHouse™
1663 Liberty Drive
Bloomington, IN 47403
www.authorhouse.com
Phone: 1-800-839-8640

Published by AuthorHouse   03/19/2012

ISBN: 978-1-4678-8983-4 (sc)
ISBN: 978-1-4678-8984-1 (e)

Contents

This book is dedicated to the memory of my father
who taught me to be patient, persevere
and strive towards worthy goals.

About the author

Fayaz Shah has extensive senior sales, marketing and commercial experience, having worked for some of the most admired healthcare companies in the world. He has managed businesses and teams across UK, Europe and Middle East. He has coached and supported many sales professionals to aspire and achieved their personal goals.

He holds Bachelor of Science from Manchester (UK), a Diploma in Marketing from Chartered Institute of Marketing and an MBA from University of Warwick (UK).

Author's acknowledgements

Thanks to the many hundreds of sales representatives that I have worked with around the world. Their interactions, passion and enthusiasm are in the heart of this book.

My sincere gratitude to my friend and colleague Nadine Nehme for her encouragement, comments and feedback throughout the writing process and thanks to all who have discussed success ideas with me over the years.

Introduction

Be not afraid of growing slowly; be afraid only of standing still.

Chinese Proverb

The healthcare industry has provided many attractive opportunities for many of today's industry leaders. For many aspiring sales professionals, sales opportunities within healthcare companies have been an attractive option from growing pharmaceutical, medical equipment, and OTC (over the counter) sectors over the past thirty years. The increase in government health expenditure and an ageing population in Western markets and Japan as well as an increase in the private sectors in developing countries have contributed to this growth. Multinational companies (MNC) have enjoyed strong performances from patent protected brands. This in turn has meant they have been able to offer attractive benefit packages and more employment security compared with other sectors.

The healthcare sales role used to be fairly straightforward: sales representatives were given a defined sales and territory target with well known brands in therapy and market areas having few competitors, little or no governmental cost pressures, easy access to key customers, prescribers and buyers. It was easy to differentiate and more often brand recall could be sufficient in most cases to generate additional sales volumes.

Over the past decade, there have been pressures on healthcare services with larger numbers of people being treated and living longer and this has had a direct bearing on the expenditure in government hospitals and clinics. The competitive environment has been increasing steadily and this has presented opportunities for small and medium size companies to enter markets previously dominated by MNC. This is the current situation in developed as well as the emerging markets. This has enabled increasing product choice for customers generating sizeable cost savings as many of the small companies have a more simplified cost base structure and an undifferentiated product offering and they can focus on price alone when submitting tender proposals or discussing strategic health economic outcomes. Healthcare reforms in many nations has been increasing influenced by patient and advocacy groups but also at the same time more administration and paperwork for physicians, prescribers and buyers, reducing the time available to meet sales representatives. This in turn increases expectations upon sales representatives who desire to be truly successful and stay ahead of competition. Qualities such as tenacity, perseverance and focus will be sought.

Despite the current market complexity and the pace of change, with which we have all become accustomed to, hiring and retaining quality sales professionals remains cornerstone for most healthcare companies' sales and marketing operations. Individuals who have the right skill set and attitude will remain in high demand and can expect improved chances of career development.

Healthcare companies have needed to make tough decisions on the required makeup and structure of sales operations. In recent years this has contributed to sizeable job losses in many key markets for many good sales professionals and undoubtedly some anxiety for others. So what are the key areas that successful sales professionals in today's environment should think and focus their attention upon that will lead to a successful career?

The ideas in this book are based on hard-won experience and knowledge. I have worked with some of the most admired companies in the world. I have been fortunate enough to meet many inspiring sales professionals from many nationalities. The one key theme linking them all was that they all wanted more success.

Sales Representatives have a challenging role. The typical day will involve having to think about hitting sales targets, getting the right call rates, gaining access to key customers through receptionist gatekeepers, battling for parking space, getting stuck in traffic jams, beating competitors to the call. After a day in the field, arriving home to read numerous emails, entering daily calls in the CRM system and then planning tomorrow . . . with the possibility of an evening speaker meeting. These daily challenges will drive the motivated individual to excel to new heights of achievement and in the process add to self development. There is constant pressure from modern pace of change coming both from the external as well as internal environment. Keeping abreast of these changes adds to the complexity.

The surety to success is taking personal ownership and responsibility for your territory and managing it as if it is your own business: one that develops sequentially, driven by your desire to excel and one which can be held accountable and is run professionally. Having the right skills and knowledge with an appreciation of how to apply this effectively is essential.

Satisfaction and enjoying the role are important ingredients. Along the journey as you build your knowledge and skills, your profile will be raised and this will help you achieve your longer term goals both within the role and toward future career aspirations.

How to use this book

This book has been written to help you by addressing the core areas that will contribute to your success as sales professional. In particular, topics such as career development and performance management are often not given enough focus and in many cases, they 'just happen'. The aim is to deepen your understanding in vital areas as well as awareness of the practical implications that should guide you towards your desired goals and objectives.

The book is organised into eight parts. The first four tackle the important aspects of your daily role, laying out some key points that should be helpful. This is followed by a detailed look at teamwork as so often this is an area not given due attention and yet so vital to most project work. The final three parts address your individual development starting with performance reviews through to career and you as an individual.

I am assuming you are a busy person. With that in mind I want you to read this book, so I have kept it short and written in a style that is practical and easy to read. I have put extra emphasis on areas from personal experience such as customer management and performance reviews, which will add value to your work and personal development. Let this book be your personal coach in areas that you want extra help with. Everyone one has a different learning style, some will find written word useful yet others frameworks and illustrations. I have endeavoured to achieve a balance in this book so that it will have the widest appeal. I am also conscious that many sales professionals especially in the healthcare industry will be well read and many will be in possession of MBA qualifications. I have limited the use of standard templates and frameworks to those that you will find effective and practical.

As is often the case, theories on sales skills and territory management are simple, it is the practical application that is hard and that is the reason you will see many practical points as well as coaching tips spread across the book. Hopefully the suggestions, ideas and frameworks will help you.

Part One Excelling in sales

The will to win, the desire to succeed, the urge to reach your full potential . . .
these are the keys that will unlock the door to personal excellence

Eddie Robinson

Sound, applicable and practical sales skills are essential in gaining the right outcome from your customers. Good habits once learned will stay with you throughout your career and will be invaluable in all circumstances. This chapter looks at how you can build your sales skills with emphasis on the sales call process and the role of sales training in your development. The application of your skills during face to face and meetings is further explored.

As with any job, you need the right tools to do it effectively. Selling skills are fundamental building blocks for your ongoing success. This is one area where companies will continue to allocate resources so as to have a fully trained sales force. Sales skills training start from the moment that you begin your career and continue throughout. Your needs will continue to evolve depending on the prevailing challenges and product mix.

Your sales skills will always be a reflection of your personality after all the role is about personal interactions with your customers. Whenever you want to build up your skill base ensure that it feels natural and right in the *way you express yourself best.* That way it will become more easily embedded and easy to apply in sales calls.

Dedicated sales training facilities exist in virtually all companies although resources available can vary a lot. Part of the cost of maintaining a successful sales force is consumed by sales training departments, often as either a separate department or incorporated into Sales or Human Resources. Sales trainers can be assigned to specific teams, product or therapy areas or can work across multiple areas. The determining factors will be the size of the organisation, product and market complexity and the size and structure of the field sales force.

Role of sales and training department

The purpose of sales and skills training is to equip the sales force with effective sales skills which will help them make an impact in front of the customer, to achieve their desired results target and develop their capabilities to aspire to higher challenges. Sales training, therefore, plays a critical role in supporting performance metrics and sales force development needs.

The key components of the sales call should be evaluated by the sales trainers to help monitor and improve the call quality and highlight areas for further coaching and development, some of the responsibility can be taken over by the direct line manager.

Figure 1.1 shows the two areas of focus for sales trainers.

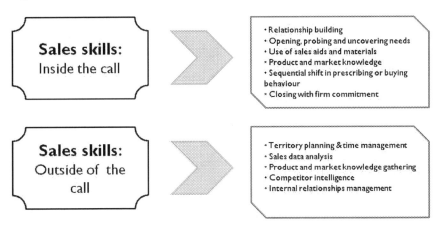

Sales skills:
Inside the call

- Relationship building
- Opening, probing and uncovering needs
- Use of sales aids and materials
- Product and market knowledge
- Sequential shift in prescribing or buying behaviour
- Closing with firm commitment

Sales skills:
Outside of the call

- Territory planning & time management
- Sales data analysis
- Product and market knowledge gathering
- Competitor intelligence
- Internal relationships management

Figure 1.1: Sales skills summary

Sales trainers should be aware of the needs of reps both in front of the customer and also in equipping them in preparing, planning and executing their sales strategies outside the call.

Sales and training structure

Sales training is the most significant area of development especially for those new to selling or their chosen industry. Whilst it is true that some individuals will display a natural flair and can readily demonstrate ability to interact well in front of the customer, for majority learning the mechanics through sales training is the normal route to personal sales skills development. Sales training can add value to your skills development. The process starts with evaluating your needs and determining how to link these into portfolio and customer outcome priorities.

Customer satisfaction is the key priority. Sales training should be designed with customer outcomes in mind. It is the role of the Sales

Trainer to train you to gain access and perform at your best during the calls.

It is important to appreciate that there will always be some areas of common interest between you and the customer (see figure 1.2). Addressing them will help to address the needs of the customer and remember that there will always be limited time, resources and access so each and every call has to count with the right balance between technical and product knowledge backed up by effective sales skills.

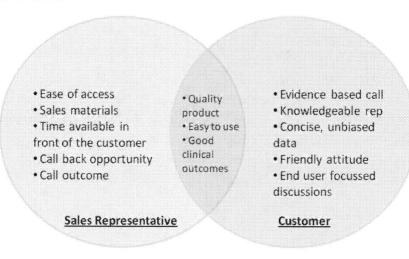

* Ease of access
* Sales materials
* Time available in front of the customer
* Call back opportunity
* Call outcome

* Quality product
* Easy to use
* Good clinical outcomes

* Evidence based call
* Knowledgeable rep
* Concise, unbiased data
* Friendly attitude
* End user focussed discussions

Sales Representative   **Customer**

Figure 1.2: Matching needs in the sales call

Do remember that the sales training department are there to help you. They will have their own metrics and to deliver both the right number of programmes.

The quality of training will depend on a number of factors:

* Aligned reporting and team structure which will achieve optimal coverage and support

- Sufficient number of trainers to meet the training needs of the region—this directly affects the availability of sales trainers in the field
- Having competent sales trainers: individuals with required depth of experience and skills, ideally located such that they have equal access to field and head office staff

It is fair to say that there is no one structure or model of sales training that would be suitable for every company. The determinant factors that ultimately affect how well training is organised, delivered and continually developed include:-

- *Training Department legacy.* Some companies have historically put in sizeable investment and have well established and developed training departments.
- *Sales training reporting structure and focus.* Clearly a training department that is integrated into HR function will have a different outlook and emphasis compared with a similar one reporting into Sales Management or dedicated Commercial Excellence department. The former may have more focus on soft skills such as communication styles, negotiations and leadership development whereas the latter may concentrated entirely on sales skills that make a critical difference to sales performance.
- *Sales training scope and focus.* This will depend on allocated budgets, headcount and the depth and breadth of activities involved.

Skills development focus

Sales trainers have an important role in developing and enhancing sales skills. Their time is usually divided between classroom training and field based training. The key goal is to equip you with the skills that affect your performance in front of the customer.

There are a number of areas where the sales trainer can add value:

- *First training programme:* the key issue here is to be able to set the right tone and company's expectation levels. This programme could feature entirely novices or experienced sales professionals joining from other companies or industries or a combination of both. It is the role of the sales trainers' to bring everyone to the same level of understanding and to achieve a level of uniformity in the required skills levels. These programmes can be up to 4 weeks in duration.
- *Product and knowledge update meetings.* These will tend to be shorter on a need basis as well as scheduled in conjunction with product and marketing managers throughout the year depending on the product and marketing campaign cycle.

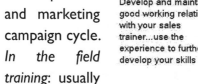

Coach's Tip

Develop and maintain a good working relationship with your sales trainer...use the experience to further develop your skills

- *In the field training:* usually a combination of local sales meetings and field visits accompanying the sales representative during calls made to customers.
- *National or Regional conferences:* there will be slots in the agenda devoted to skills development and are also an ideal opportunity for role play practice.

Sale training can be delivered in class room style teaching format with a good dose of PowerPoint presentations, group exercises and role plays. In the field this training can be extended to practical setting, usually involving smaller numbers.

Elements of sales training can be delivered through external vendors especially in smaller organisations. This can be on a need basis or part of longer term agreement on a package range.

Sales call process for individual face to face meetings

Most sales professionals will be very familiar with the conventional flow and components of a face to face sales call with a customer. The before, during and after view of sales call is useful way to ensure there is adequate preparation before the call, maximising sales opportunities during the call and clear follow up actions after the call.

Figure 1.3 illustrates the typical questions to consider at each stage. It is important to note that the whole process should be fluid and seamless one.

The important points to consider in planning, preparing and executing sales call are:-

- Preparing well before the call makes a lot of sense.
- Up to date buying patterns, prescribing data, competitor activities, profile of the customer etc will mean the call be well focussed and directed. This process doesn't need to take too long for familiar or regular customers.

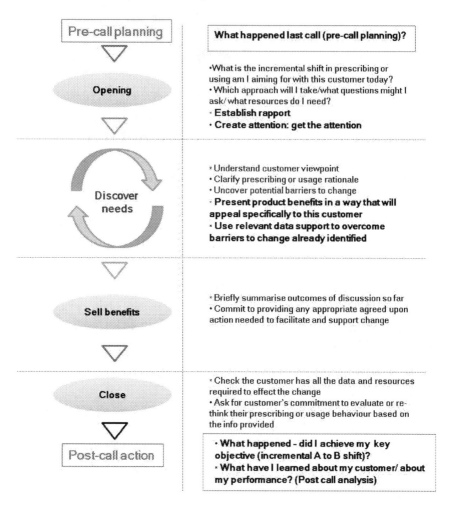

Figure 1.3: Typical sales call model

Get into the habit of asking **SMART** (specific, measurable, achievable, realistic and time bound) questions, this will help you to achieve meaningful answers.

- Establishing rapport and uncovering needs mean you will need to connect well with your customer. This is not the same as having sound relationships because on this particular occasion, the customer could be distracted or has many issues on his mind, limiting the attention span. Sensing the temperature and context of the call should prevent you from going into an auto pilot mode and will require adjustments to the call such as shortening the opening, focussing on one specific need and settling on one clear outcome. These factors will also be relevant during short calls, those of less than ten minutes duration.

- You should establish a clear need in the mind of the customer. This will clearly direct the call to your desired outcome. This all starts with a clear mind set, logical flow, SMART questions and the appropriate use of market and product knowledge.

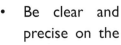

Coach's Tip

Asking the right questions and an effective close are two key areas to focus on

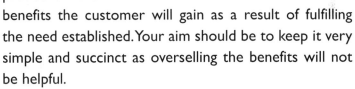

- Be clear and precise on the benefits the customer will gain as a result of fulfilling the need established. Your aim should be to keep it very simple and succinct as overselling the benefits will not be helpful.

- Getting a clear commitment to buying more, prescribing more or ordering more will be the natural outcome of the preceding two stages.

- The outcomes of the sales call need to be recorded into the call reporting format that is currently used by your company. Try to get into a habit of recording activity data on a daily basis if possible and avoid leaving it all to the end of the working week. Relying on memory may not provide the most accurate picture upon which to base future calls.

Sales call process for group meetings

The key difference in group meetings is that you may not have the same opportunity to discuss the required level of detail on an individual basis but on the other hand you can cover more customers in a single meeting. To be impactful, it is important to be well focussed on the messages that you would like to get across and the outcome that is sought.

Having SMART objectives certainly helps as well as adjusting your strategy in relation to the size of the group and type of meeting:-

- *Small group presentations:* with a group size 5-7 this can be an excellent opportunity to promote your brands and have a lively interactive presentation. The setting can vary from large or small meeting rooms to much smaller locations. Whatever the setting, make sure you adequately cover the following areas:

  - ✧ If at all possible, check the room and setting beforehand to be totally familiar with all the layout
  - ✧ Professional audio visuals that can be seen and heard by all the participants very clearly
  - ✧ Maintain good eye contact across the room and ensure you project a clear tone
  - ✧ Prepare and ready all the materials and data that you would like to hand out or leave with the group. This may be better at the end of your presentation so as to avoid any distractions during the presentation itself. By all means use the data for any defined reference that may arise from the discussion

✦ Allow opportunity for questions and discussions but try to keep the theme and direction that you desire after clearly addressing any specific questions or issues that arise from the group

✦ Try to gain specific commitment or outcome with a clear action to follow up after the meeting

- *Mid size group meetings*: for group size 8-12 in number. Controlling the course of discussion and outcome can be a challenge. It will be helpful to plan ahead on the flow of discussion envisaged, the key individuals to be seen, the key messages that must be given and a clear sense of desired outcome. If you want to explore any particular aspect with anyone individually, take the opportunity to request additional time after your group meeting but keep the request smart and definitive and try to avoid treating the individual meeting just like an individual appointment at the individual's place of work. They may have other commitments after the meeting and it is wise to build rapport that can be subsequently followed up at face to face calls.

- *Large group and exhibition or booth managed meetings*: chances are you will meet many more customers but it is unlikely that you will have the opportunity to discuss in meaningful depth details relating to your brand or company. Instead there will be plenty of opportunities for follow up calls, information dissemination and good PR for your brand and product. To get the most out of these meetings, the following points will be helpful:-

✦ Keep to time discipline. If the meeting is organised by an external company or organisation, there will be time slots during the day when most delegates will visit booths and during these busy periods you will need to devote maximum attention and energy.

✧ Keep your stand or display areas neat and tidy which may not be easy when there are large number of delegates and many individuals keen to take brochures, leaflets and other information as well as company or brand giveaway items. Keep the stock at an acceptable level and replenish as needed.

✧ Note down all the relevant delegate information in a note book and keep all visiting cards together out of way behind the stand etc where you can retrieve later. Follow up on any commitments made if at all possible a week following the meeting, this way it will still be fresh.

✧ If you are working as part of a team managing the company stand, ensure there is clear communication over timings for coverage and managing the stand.

✧ If you are responsible for organising the stand, prepare well in advance so that all the relevant materials are available, the artwork for the stand is completed and all the practical and logistical tasks are covered.

Follow up promptly as this discipline will prove invaluable in getting the best outcome from each and every meeting that you organise or attend. Swift action on commitments made during meetings will enhance your credibility in the eye of the customer. To accomplish this you must be well organised and methodical in the follow up actions.

Using Call Reporting Management (CRM) tools

The vast majority of sales professionals today will have access to a CRM system. Embracing the usage of a CRM system to systematically record your performance is vital and beneficial in helping you to shape your activities and to indicate shortfalls in territory management that will help you to be more successful. The system must be used regularly and consistently to derive true benefits.

The accuracy of call reports should be at the heart of a CRM system. Most reps will use the post call facility to record outcomes but less will log pre-call objectives. In an era that is moving towards Account Management model, planning and organisation skills become increasingly important. Of course any system relies on personal honesty, how honest are you in your call reporting? Over the years, research has shown healthcare sales professionals to be surprisingly honest about their dishonesty! The key areas to focus on giving the right information are:

- Number of customers seen face to face
- Number of attendees at meetings
- Number of products detailed or discussed
- Delivery of key messages for all detailed products

So what was once perceived as a monitoring and policing tool should now be regarded as an opportunity to plan and manage your territory professionally. This can be helpful in further discussions during customer calls or help segment customers to identify high potential accounts.

The CRM system should easy to use. Ideally you should have a portable device that is easy to carry and store with ample battery life to support any work that you can do on the road. Functional improvements to the customer database and assistance in segmenting and profiling customers are critical components but despite any technological frustrations

Coach's Tip

Learn to use all of the functions of your CRM system to help your planning and record keeping

that you may encounter, CRMs are helpful in managing the increasing complexity and sometimes sophistication in your customer data.

Ongoing learning

Learning should be an ongoing process throughout your career. The process starts with an innate desire to develop and grow as an individual and to excel in your sales career, making the transition to promotion smoother. As you begin a new role, having a disciplined approach to learning will help you to quickly prioritise your key tasks and get hold of the desired information.

Many large MNCs as well as medium size companies invest in training and development. This means that for many areas of development, you should have access to a wealth of training and skills development material internally. Quite often the issue is locating the learning material. Depending on the structure of your organisation, the best places to look can include:-

- Human Resource Dept—personal and career development in particular. Historic learning tools and data can be found on the appropriate intranet site.
- Sales training dept containing current and previous training materials
- Company intranet resources

Acquiring and using knowledge

The amount of information and knowledge expected from sales representatives is high with expertise expected in a number of areas: in depth clinical knowledge, marketing and sales tactics, pricing, scientific claims, technical data and health economics.

To meet this challenge, you need to keep the availability of information at your finger tips. Learning that can be intertwined within the role is most effective. All too often fact based learning is conducted through classroom style training which can often be removed from the working environment.

In general, healthcare industry has not fully developed alternative ways to deliver pertinent knowledge. Now with newer portable devices such as Apple's ipad make it much easier to enable the field based individual to complete their learning modules. The key is manageability by head office and flexibility for the field user, enabling the access of vital information between appointments and reducing time off road.

Part one Summary

- ✧ Sound selling skills are fundamental to your role and you must continue to and nurture develop them
- ✧ Sales training department will support your skills development; utilise the resources available
- ✧ Selling skills must be matched by high proficiency in product and market knowledge
- ✧ Face to face meetings will provide opportunities to explore your product's value proposition in detail
- ✧ Group meetings will help you to reach wider customer base but they must be followed up to be effective

- ✧ Use the sales call model and decide which steps you need further work on and put an action plan to achieve this
- ✧ Ongoing learning is important and to be really effective it must be applied in the field

Part Two Managing your territory and customers

What we think or what we know or what we believe is, in the end, of little consequence.
The only consequence is what we sow

John Ruskin

Managing your territory or area of responsibility effectively will be critical to your success. This requires some discipline and a methodical approach. Managing your customers well will require a deal of hard work and effort but the relationships you make, the quality of discussions that you have and how you utilise your available resources will determine your ultimate success.

For many representatives, the opportunity to work outside the office environment on their own territory is a major attraction. The daily routine will not be fixed, there will be a lot of variety in the day and no two days are likely to be identical. This remoteness from head office or district sales office will require a degree of self discipline to achieve desired sales success because there will be endless list of admin tasks that will require your attention and through which you will also be evaluated against your role effectiveness. Let's consider the key focus areas for your success.

Managing time effectively

Simply put, there are not enough hours in your typical day to achieve everything. Being organised and disciplined around managing your daily schedule is very important. This will require good organisation and degree of discipline.

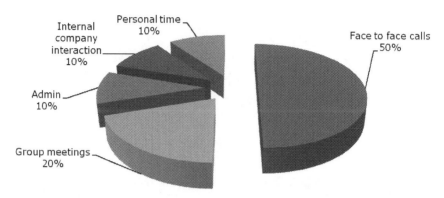

Figure 2.1: Daily activities time split

Figure 2.1 shows the time split for an average day. This is an ideal split with a focus on customer interaction without neglecting the vital admin and dealing with your company colleagues. If we assume a maximum ten hours available, devoting half of that to face to face meetings makes good sense where you will make the most impact on your sales performance.

Time management is a really useful skill to have. It is about understanding your key priorities and then arranging your daily schedule, with some flexibility to include unexpected or last minute tasks. In an average day, there will be high degree of time fragmentation, sometimes the time devoted to seeing customers may have to be altered, extra time spent in traffic or parking delays can be irritating. In general, your time commitment should be centred on the following priorities:-

- *Face to face customer calls* both appointments and spec calls in line with your overall call rate objectives. Think about the location for the meeting and plan in extra time depending on the time of the day and other practical issues.

- *Customer group meetings*—these can take place at breakfast, lunch, afternoon or evening time. Depending on the nature and size of the group, prior preparation is likely to be essential. The location can also be critical to success. It is vitally important that you arrive at the venue in good time ahead of your customers so that any last minute organisation can take place 'behind the scenes' rather than in front of your customers. Ensure that you allow adequate time to plan for each meeting and to take into account questions and discussions that may be necessary. If the meeting is to be followed by sit down meal, then the timing should be agreed in advance with the restaurant or hotel so that such issues do not take up valuable time you would rather spend with your customers.
- *Admin work* affect your activities—these can directly affect your customer interaction or can be internal company related admin such approval forms, expense claims etc. Prioritise according to importance and urgency. Plan these activities into weekly schedule so that you do not miss any important deadline. Try to incorporate sufficient time for any approvals of forms submitted etc so they do not interrupt your schedule.
- *Internal company interactions* can be important but really depends on who you are dealing with and the relevance to your work. For routine and regular contacts, it is a good idea to ask them for preferred time which is mutually convenient. Returning calls can also be made during the day or can be left to the end, this depends on the urgency and nature of the call as well as your personal preference. Dealing promptly with your line

manager and direct customer queries is always helpful and if practiced consistently will make you very reliable. When you are dealing with your colleagues it is good to exercise some discipline, so that you can focus on the key discussion points first and foremost and other talking points do not distract your attention.

- *Personal time* is about recognising and including your needs such as lunch, personal family commitments etc. It is important to be able to plan at least one short break during the day so that you can maintain your energy levels. Your performance will be affected by not eating well and arriving late. Don't underestimate your energy requirements as you work through your daily tasks as customer meetings alone will require your full concentration. Always remember there will be external aspects that you cannot control such as the weather and the traffic so there is no point in worrying. Maintain good customer contacts and communications so that any delays beyond your control can be managed effectively.

In terms of managing your tasks, it is worth categorising these into distinct categories and within each prioritise according to need. Clearly some tasks will be repetitive; others will need one time effort.

Coach's Tip

Have some discipline and maintain control over the way you manage your daily tasks...learn to say 'no' where appropriate

Customer activities	Planning tasks
☑ Request for data	☑ Weekly & monthly schedule
☑ Booking appointments and meetings	☑ External expert management
☑ Conference attendance	☑ Joint team activities
☑ Arranging speakers etc	☑ Sales data gathering
Company related tasks	Admin tasks
☑ Sales meetings	☑ Approval forms
☑ Field visit requests	☑ Payment of invoices
☑ Marketing intelligence	☑ Organising promotional materials
☑ Expenses, other paperwork	☑ Online learning

Figure 2.2 Tasks broken down into categories and prioritised based on business needs

Customer management

Managing your customers must be your number one priority. It can be challenging but if done well ultimately rewarding part of the job because it is the personal interactions that make all the critical difference to your performance and through which you can achieve personal satisfaction.

Customer selection

Selecting the right customer and calling on them at the right frequency makes logical sense. Let us first understand the key concepts used in selecting appropriate customers:

- *Target customer*: the chosen customer from total list identified as being key target for product use, prescribing or ordering your product. Ideally the profile and background of this target should match certain criteria such as therapy and product knowledge, sales history, strong advocate.

- *Customer segmentation*: defining the customer into smaller cluster so that within your target group you have identified most high potential customers. This list will directly affect your activities and needs some careful evaluation and input.

The method chosen to build up target list within the right segments depends upon the nature of your product. For older late life cycle products, there should be sufficient usage data available internally as well as externally published. Here the key issue is to re-evaluate in light of any customer or market changes that affect your territory. For newly launched products, customer profiling and list build up should have been made by your marketing department but in therapy or product areas which are new to your company, building an accurate database should be jointly conducted by sales and marketing teams.

Avoid calling on customers just because you happen to be in the 'area'. Some customers will prefer a more frequent calling pattern than others but use your judgement wisely.

Once selected, ensure that your customer target list is completed within your call reporting software so that activity performance can be measured accurately.

Figure 2.3 Be prepared and have the right focus for your calls

Relationship development

Products don't sell themselves; the critical difference is made by people. Essential to your success will be the relationships that you develop and use

Coach's Tip
_____

Develop and value the relationships you make with your customers...your long term success depends upon them

effectively. Your sales, organisational and business skills must be matched by robust relationships, particularly with key customers. The relationships we are referring to are professional business relationships that are underpinned by high degree of trust, understanding and mutual respect. This is backed up by excellent rapport, good communication and regular contact. This is an area where you must work hard to establish your credentials and just like any other business skill, it needs hard work, focus and attention to detail. Relationships can take time to develop but can be easily broken by one inappropriate act, which means that you have to remain vigilant and direct your energies. Quite often your competitor product may very closely match your features and benefits and it can be your established relationships that can make all the difference.

So what are the important aspects that you should consider in establishing, developing and maintaining your customer relationships?

- *Impact of the first impression*: the first time you meet your customer must be seen as an important meeting. Creating the right first impression is important not only in job interviews but in the image that is formed in the mind of your customers. Follow the usual relevant meeting rules (see fig 3.4). Keep the discussion relevant and succinct so that you can develop rapport at the next meeting. Leave with a good lasting impression

Figure 2.4: Important first meeting with a customer

- *Linking with the personality*: it is important to appreciate that your customers will have similar fears and emotions that you have. Understanding the personality differences and adjusting your communication style to match it is important so that you can be most effective during your meetings. In the field of psychology there is a considerable volume written on this subject. There are many theories and no doubt you may have attended courses on 'personality types'. The following is a brief highlight of two of the most popular theories, these underpin much of contemporary personality thinking:

  ◇ At its basic, the early Greeks defined human nature into four groups. Hippocrates for example, described four temperaments to the human body fluid (figure 2.5). So you can see some people who are action-oriented (they're "Artisans"), some people are ideal-oriented (they're "Idealists"), some are theory-oriented (they're "Rationalists") and some people are fact-oriented (they're "Guardians")

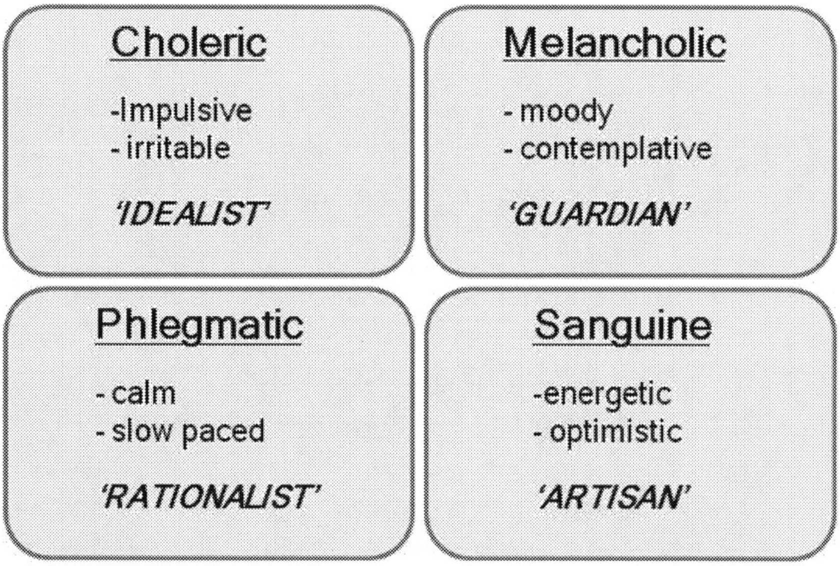

Choleric	Melancholic
-Impulsive - irritable *'IDEALIST'*	- moody - contemplative *'GUARDIAN'*
Phlegmatic	Sanguine
- calm - slow paced *'RATIONALIST'*	-energetic - optimistic *'ARTISAN'*

Figure 2.5: Hipprocates description of human personality as body fluids

✧ Carl Jung formed four basic functions of the 'psychological man'. At its basic, you should be able to identify with opposite personality types, introvert and extrovert. Figure 2.6 shows the basic attitudes and that every individual has one dominant function at birth. You will see some customers naturally falling into these personality types, each requiring a different communication approach. Look out for the language and expression of customers and adjust your approach accordingly.

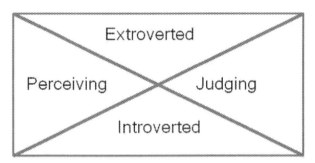

Figure 2.6: Carl Jung's description of functions and attitudes describing personalities

✧ It is important to be aware of your customers' personality types as well as your own preference: some customers will prefer a lot of detail in the discussion; others will prefer more top line data. At the beginning of your relationship take a cautious approach and make your meetings balanced and coherent both in content and style. As you get to know your customers better, adjust according to personality types and preferences.

✧ Building up profile for a new customer will be helpful. By all means start by asking other sales representatives and colleagues who may know the individual. It is important that such advice is taken within context of their knowledge and relationship. Use the information wisely but form your own opinions and knowledge from firsthand experience.

✧ Take particular care and sound judgement when discussing subjects outside your professional call content particularly personal or opinions about their colleagues etc. There may be an appropriate time and place but you will likely to dampen your professional image which you have worked so hard to create. Needless to say sensitive subjects relating to sex, culture and politics should be avoided, remember you are acting in your professional capacity and also representing your company in front of the customer, so think carefully before speaking.

Coach's Tip

Take the time to understand your customers' personalities so that you can make a better connection

• *Customer access:* healthcare professionals are busy people with packed agendas, conflicting appointments, patients to see, emergencies to deal with etc. Some customers will have to operate a rigid appointments system outside which it may not be possible to gain access whilst others will have loose arrangements preferring sales reps to call on spec. If you are unsure, ask other reps or call the clinic or practice in advance. In some cases you may be faced with an experienced gate keeper, likely to be a receptionist or a departmental secretary. It is worth developing a good rapport and working relationship with this individual who can be very helpful in gaining access as well as conveying useful information when required. Some customers can respond to seeing you with an access item. It is important for long term relationship that you use this access route appropriately, i.e. if the customer is unable to see you but has requested that you leave it, you must be prepared to do so.

- *Frequency of contact:* your customer target list will also have a frequency of contact value attached to each customer or groups of customers. This indicative guide can be very helpful in shaping your calling list and agenda for each week and month. The required frequency of contact will be dependent on a number of factors:

  - ✧ The nature and complexity of your product portfolio. An 'uncomplicated' product in a heavy noise driven market with many competitors means more frequent visits than a specialist or niche area with few competitors.

  - ✧ Promotional cycle may require additional visits to communicate new support material etc.

  - ✧ Customer preferences: access via set appointments can be restrictive. Other customers may state their preferred calling frequency. In most cases, the relationship you have will determine the frequency of call. Where you are unsure ask the customer and work within that guideline. In any case it is a good idea to maintain good frequency so as to ensure the customer keeps you and your products in mind. The key to success is to have a good valid reason for your contact visit and that you can demonstrate you are adding value on each visit.

- *Customer service:* don't underestimate the support element of your role. Professionally responding to valid requests for information or meeting attendance etc will be highly appreciated in the eyes of your customers. Being seen as helpful, co-operative and willing to go the 'extra mile' can help to distinguish you from your competitors. Exercise your judgement on the nature of requests made (new product data, meeting request, local data etc) and professionally and politely decline any that can potentially compromise your position and relationship.

Business planning

Having a customer target list is a good start, but you need to go beyond and evaluate the business potential and the return on investment you can expect. This can be done either at individual customer level or on an account level, depending on how many customers and accounts you have and the complexity of your product. The level of detail that is required will ultimately depend on the type of information that is needed and how useful it will be to grow sales. Go into as much detail as is needed to gain full understanding of your key customers and accounts, what influences them and ultimately what drives your sales numbers.

External analysis

You can start by analysing the bigger picture and putting into this context your own territory. At this stage you can consider the available business opportunities and ask yourself if you have all the needed resources at your disposal such as adequate activity budget, promotional materials, meetings support etc. You should go beyond just analysis of sales and competitor data, take into account the external environment in which you work in. A good starting point is the PEST model (Political, Economic, Socio and Technological influences), which may be familiar to you. This should help you examine more widely external market influences on your work and can also present business opportunities. Take a 2-3 year horizon in the future when you are undertaking this analysis. Figure 2.7 shows an example of such analysis. Try to take into account every conceivable point relating to each category.

Have a close look at the factors you have identified and rank these according to the potential to impact your business both negative and positive.

P	E
• Healthcare reforms • Patient groups influence • Healthcare spending • Health dept powerbase • Healthcare priorities • Local healthcare policies	• Healthcare expenditure as % GDP • Economic environment • Healthcare budget constraints • Expenditure provision • Key economic indicators • Budget planning cycle • Budget review process
S	T
• Population dynamics • Education • National and Regional living standards • Cultural impact on healthcare • Equality of healthcare provision	• Electronic automation healthcare processes • Analytical and decision making tools • Technological changes in healthcare provision • Electronic promotional support

Figure 2.7: Typical PEST analysis

Competitor analysis

Having access to quality competitor information and market intelligence is really worth the effort. This can include published and publically available material as well as what you are able to collate through your discussions with key customers, suppliers, your colleagues etc.

Make a thorough assessment of all key competitor products as possible with the data at your disposal, making sound judgement particularly on the following points:-

- How long has the product been in the market on your territory, is it newly launched (6 months to one year) or an existing brand that has been available on your territory for over one year?
- What is the market penetration? Do the competitor products enjoy a low or high market share relative to your own brand?

Figure 2.8 shows an example of the sales tactics that you should think about when you have made your assessment. It is worthwhile looking at the issue within context of the overall market taking into account market dynamics and tactics that affect your colleagues' territories, how does your territory compare? Are there any specific issues that are particular to your territory that cannot be replicated elsewhere or is your territory reflecting a national trend?

If the performance of your competitor products is similar to your colleagues, you may want to consider working together (possibly with the involvement of the relevant marketing personnel) and collectively devise strategy to face the competition.

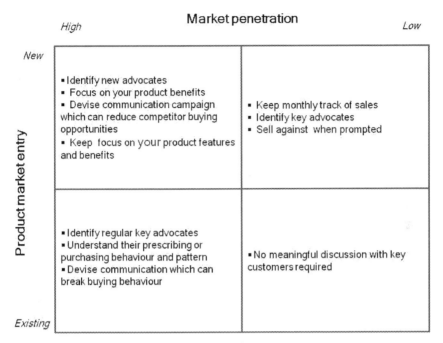

Figure 2.8 Competitor product analysis

Sales forecasting

This need not be a very difficult exercise, just a realistic appraisal of your product taking into account market trends, buying patterns, prescribing behaviour and

Coach's Tip

Maintain a balance between short and long term business horizon - keep a key eye on market developments that affect your business

known and predictable market dynamics. Include whenever possible price changes, pack size alterations, new indications etc so that the analysis is more meaningful. This projection can span 18 months to 2 year horizon and can be updated every six months. Put together a workable spreadsheet as reference and review in line with changes in your territory.

Account level analysis

The more you understand the context of your business at the individual account or customer level, the more effective you will be at realising the full potential that will contribute to the growth in sales that you can realistically expect.

When you are analysing your accounts or key customers, it can be helpful to break this into three areas of focus:-

1. Business potential: how much business are you currently generating from this customer or account (which may be a group of customers) and how much more can be gained? Try to quantify this:

    i.   Patient list size
    ii.   Competitor sales
    iii. Population served
    iv.   Total market size or potential

2. Relationship: the key question is, 'can you classify your current relationships?' The main attributes to take into account are access and frequency of contact. Clearly if your relationship makes it easy to access at the desired frequency, this will be part of your competitive advantage. Think of relationship in wider context of your account or customer. Learn to understand the relationships between all the key decision makers but also take into account other key influencers in your pursuit to increase sales. Figure 2.9 is an attempt to demonstrate, using a fictitious account that you should be aware of the level of influence each customer within an account makes and also where the decision making power lies.

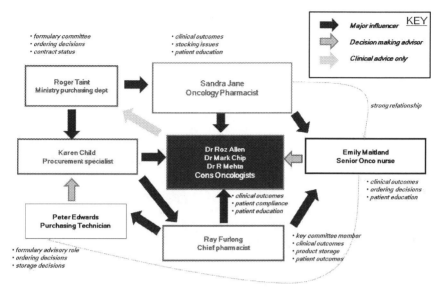

Figure 2.9: Build strong relationships with all key customers that can affect your sales

3. Security: how secure are your sales from this customer or account? If the competitor representative can easily substitute their products, this will weaken your capability, undermine your activity and will require additional effort. There will be a number of factors that should be considered:

 i. quality of your calls and the impact you can make in each call or meeting

 ii. price and commercial terms that affect your orders

 iii. competitor representatives' relationships and their price and commercial terms

 iv. quality of the data you use and present in an effective way

 v. key advocate support and communication in your market

 vi. external factors such as relevant articles in the media, supply chain issues, new indication of competitor product etc.

Once you have done your analysis, quantify each of the above areas and you can see visually in figure 2.10 three separate accounts.

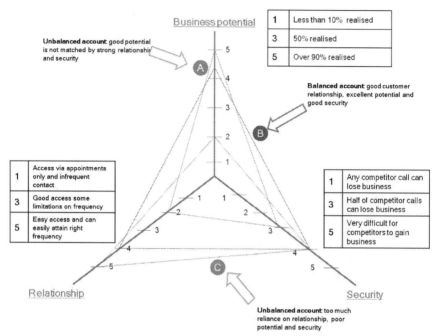

1	Less than 10% realised
3	50% realised
5	Over 90% realised

Unbalanced account good potential is not matched by strong relationship and security

Balanced account good customer relationship, excellent potential and good security

1	Access via appointments only and infrequent contact
3	Good access some limitations on frequency
5	Easy access and can easily attain right frequency

1	Any competitor call can lose business
3	Half of competitor calls can lose business
5	Very difficult for competitors to gain business

Unbalanced account too much reliance on relationship, poor potential and security

Figure 2.10: 'spider web' showing the need to have balance between business potential, relationship and security

Accounts A & C have an unbalanced approach with over reliance on potential not being matched by the relationship (A) or low potential despite good relationship (C). Account B shows a very balanced account with good potential that is supported by good access and frequency and challenging for competitors to penetrate.

Once you have undertaken the required analysis by account or customer, you can prioritise according to the additional attention you will need to pay to

Coach's Tip

Base your potential business calculations on realistic assumptions - evaluate in light of all available information

understanding business potential, relationship and security. Obtaining quantitative data around business potential should be relatively straightforward and will not take much time. Relationship building and developing as well as attention to detail around security building should be seen in mid to long term perspective. Allow yourself six months to one year to work on these areas and make step by step progress to a level you will feel comfortable.

Part three Summary

- Manage your time well by prioritising your daily tasks
- Do not neglect admin work as this can pile up and slow your progress
- Plan at least one short break in a hectic day for your personal needs
- Customer management is about selecting the right target customer (with highest potential to prescribe or use your product) and visiting them at the optimal frequency
- Work hard on developing and nurturing excellent working relationships with your customers
- Understanding the personality type of your customers will help to improve outcomes as well as assisting you in customers' critical decision making about selecting your product
- Plan your territory in some detail and take a broader view of your business to maximise the available opportunities

Part Three   Managing line manager relationships

Success in life, in anything, depends upon the number of persons that one can make himself agreeable to

Thomas Carlyle

Your line manager will have the most important influence in your role and career. Having an effective close working relationship with your line manager is essential for your skills and personal development. The first line sales manager can help to develop and shape your performance and ultimately guide your career path. This chapter looks at the role of the first line sales manager, followed by a discussion on how to effectively manage your relationship.

Field based sales activities are usually managed by first line sales managers, who invariably work their way from sales representative to this first management position. They will have first hand sales experience as well as market knowledge and the understanding of the sales process and the key success factors that affect representative performance.

Role of sales managers

The Role of First Line Sales Manager (FLSM) is pivotal to business success as well as your success, yet it is often one of the least understood roles within an organisation's sales structure. Responsible for critical decisions regarding hiring, developing, coaching and controlling the focus, direction and performance of the sales team, as well as being expected to provide vital input to a number of strategic business areas, many FLSM's are in roles for which they are often not well prepared. The reasoning can be seen by the following comparison between your role and your manager's role:

Sales Representative	First Line Sales Manager
Have clear direction and direct measures of success	Have indirect measures of success (their sales team's performance)
Have clearly defined work boundaries—execute on the sales process	Management process is often self defined without clear guidelines
Have a clear understanding of how they contribute organisational value—sales	No clear understanding outside direct contribution by sales reps
Not fond about rules and spend much of their time getting around them to serve customers	Are required to enforce the rules they once hated

Establishing a sound working relationship from the beginning of your career is essential. Manager's support can come in many ways and it will help to ensure your professional development is kept on the right track.

The role of the first line manager can be challenging. The individual has to balance many tasks:
- sales performance and market development
- on the job team and individual skills enhancement
- external customer relationship management
- internal organisation key stakeholder relationships
- managing senior line management relationship

The above list goes to show the increasing complexity and the juggling of tasks that are asked and the limitations to the available time allocation to representatives' activities. These challenges will be dependent on the size of the sales team to be managed, market and product complexity, experience mix in the team and available resources.

A highly organised sales manager will be able to prioritise his or her schedule so as to ensure there is adequate attention paid to each critical business area. It could be argued that people development should be the number one priority for a FLSM. Today, a sales manager is more of a coach than a true manager. Sales managers will bring their own management style and personality to the role and this may also dictate certain limitations to their effectiveness.

It is fair to conclude that sales managers spend considerable time on meeting the sales targets, particularly in the short term. Your input and support will be invaluable in ensuring:-

Coach's Tip

Learn to understand the demands and pressures upon your manager so that you can work more effectively

- timely placement of needed orders
- managing stock effectively at wholesale or retail level
- developing key customers
- improving market and customer access

Developing partnership

By understanding more fully and appreciating the role and pressures on your line manager, you will begin to develop a better working relationship. The following key factors are important in helping you to shape this relationship:

- better understanding of the business within your territory area: key accounts, purchase patterns, prescribing behaviours, stock turnover etc.

- clear outcome focus on sales performance
- having a 'can do' attitude and being willing to go the extra mile to achieve optimal performance
- developing and enhancing key customer relationships
- being well organised and planned
- focussed territory activities—right balance of face to face and meetings

If you can focus on the above key parameters and demonstrate your capabilities including on the job performance, this should go some way to instil a degree of confidence by your line manager in you as an individual.

Coach's Tip

Work consciously with your manager; be proactive and take the lead and demonstrate your commitment to a healthy working relationship

Creating right expectations

Doing well in your field based activities is important but not enough to have a very good working relationship with your line manager. There has to be transparency and acknowledgement on the expectations that you should have from your manager and the clear expectations your manager has of you.

In most organisations, there will be formal opportunity to have performance reviews, up to three times in the year. These official reviews can be challenging if in the interim period the quality of dialogue you develop and the areas of focus that are discussed as well as the action plans that will need to be developed are not clear because the end of year review should not bring up unexpected surprises.

Use the available contact opportunities you have with your line manager to continually review a number of areas that will impact upon your working relationship:-

- Ongoing support in your activities: here you need to be clear in your mind the level and type of support that you are requesting. Focus on areas that your line manager can have the most impact. This could include meeting key customers, request for additional order quantity or supply or putting together a meeting agenda and presentation etc.
- Your line manager should seek and provide opportunities for your exposure to senior management particularly if this relates to a specific project for example. He or she will understand the company and will be able to articulate where the company is heading and potential openings that may come up. An excellent manager knows both the formal organisation chart as well as the informal power structure.
- In the field coaching including selective field visits to provide ongoing support and development.

Managing your expectations

What should you expect from your line manager? There should be certain basic building blocks that are part of your expectations. First and foremost your manager should be capable of initiating and completing key tasks. You should be supported in getting a winning price or a product placement in a tender bid or formulary inclusion. In addition there are other areas where you should focus your expectations:

- Strategy and performance direction should be clear and supported.
- You need to be treated with the required respect within the team and specific focus around your development needs. You need to recognise this may mean that the line manager uses his or her experience to differentiate the team by evaluating skills, their developmental needs and their team expertise.
- The need to spend quality time in relation to the competing commitments in the agenda is important. Some managers will use the lunch-and learn concept, others may prefer a weekly sit-down session; some have a regular chalk-talk schedule. But, it should always be regular and not ad hoc or an afterthought.
- For too many sales managers coaching is an interruption from the daily routine, not an essential part of it. You should insist on regular coaching sessions because for the excellent sales manager, teaching is worth the expenditure of time because they understand it has the ability to leverage their own talents in a way that case-by-case sales situation intervention never can.
- What differentiates excellent managers is the quality of their communication. They know that communication must be direct, candid, interactive and frequent. The team must belief that they are being listened to, as well as talked to. Sales reps of excellent sales managers know where their boss' stand. They often adopt an internal slang or verbal shorthand which helps them communicate ideas and issues about products, competitors, sales tactics or pricing. They treat different people according to their needs.
- Your manager should be capable of balancing the sales process (business management of orders, key customers,

sales target setting etc) and leading you and your colleagues in that process.

Do discuss with your manager if you feel he or she has been unable to gain a balance with all the various tasks that needs

Coach's Tip

Calibrating your expectations depend on good communications as well as good understanding on all key issues affecting your performance and business

attention. Be aware of the time pressure on your manager. As you can see from Figure 2.1 over a third of their time should be devoted to supporting the sales team but do bear in mind that the any sales campaigns and other pertinent issues will affect the time commitment, so discuss in light of practical circumstances.

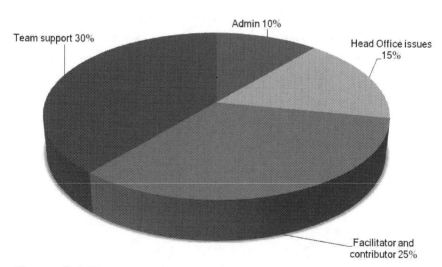

Figure 3.1: Time and effort commitment by a typical first line sales manager

The more you get to know and work with your manager, the better you will understand the individual's personality and preference. By adjusting your own ways of working to match is the beginning of an effective working relationship.

Managing critical moments

No matter how good relationship you have with your manager, there will inevitably be occasions when that relationship is tested or strained. Partly this is the nature of the industry and role you both have and mixed in will be the constant flow of challenges and personality differences.

The need to maintain continuity of support and direction is critical to your success so that you have to work hard to keep the relationship alive and working for you. There will be times when a little extra thought and effort in your relationship requires some attention:

- *Around budgeting and sales targeting setting process*—key is to understand the underlying business rationale and reasons behind the decisions. Try to actively contribute whenever the opportunity is presented
- *Team issues or conflicts*—understanding and support are important
- *Unavailability for urgent pending matters*—travel or other personal commitments could be the cause. It is important to be aware of your manager's schedule and commitment and procedure of contact in his or her absence
- *Customer relationship management*—this is especially crucial if this relates to a customer complaint of any kind. Be proactive in informing your manager providing full details and background so that appropriate action can be taken

Having the right communication channels with your manager is the key to handling the above and other issues that test the relationship. Whenever you are in doubt, ask your manager on the preferred ways of communicating and the appropriate ways to keep in touch including the frequency.

Coach's Tip

Do see the issue from your manager's viewpoint as this will help your understanding of any decision that you are unsure about

Part three Summary

- The relationship you have with your line manager is important and can determine your development path
- Get to know your manager and understand his or her role well
- Communication is the key to successful relationship; make the effort to communicate effectively and request the same from your manager
- Ensure your expectations are balanced between business management and your personal development
- Think about those critical moments when your relationship may be challenged, plan and prepare as much as possible

Part Four Product and market knowledge

A good decision is based on knowledge and not on numbers

Plato

Acquiring knowledge about your products, your company and competitors is absolutely essential. The application of this knowledge with your customers will determine your successful entry and longevity in the sales role. Learning styles vary but it is important that whatever style you have it is effective particularly when communicating with your customers. This chapter focuses on learning as a key element in your success and development.

A good grasp of technical information is essential. This will be related to your promoted products or equipment as well as competitors'. You must understand thoroughly the key attributes of your products against which you will measure competitors' offerings and upon which you will sell the benefits. You need to be seen as an expert in your particular area of focus and be able to converse with your customers on the same level. Contemporary healthcare sales professionals should be seen as respected product or device advisors, with capacity to manage any query or issue.

Knowledge management as a concept is invariably extensively discussed in most MNC healthcare companies. Many companies attempt to manage the knowledge required by sales representatives through the Regulatory, Medical and Training functions, ideally solutions that allow users to store, analyse, interpret and share information as part of coordinated process. Many companies will view the technical data you require in a wider context, not only text documents, but also non-text files such as molecular structures, gene sequence alignments, images, results tables, entry forms and other relevant information. Also included are links to key internal and external resources, discussion items, key e-mails, external search results, and status and summary reports.

Types of knowledge

Competency in front of your customer is best demonstrated through your professionalism and central to that is your knowledge about your products, your company, competitors and all the relevant technical details that can be requested and expected. Sales training skills are of course important in handling questions and objections but you must feel absolutely comfortable with every aspect of the knowledge that you acquire and you use appropriately. Figure 4.1 shows examples from three categories of knowledge which you should be thoroughly familiar with.

Product data sheet knowledge	Medical knowledge	Market knowledge
• Product delivery system • Product indication • Contraindications • Major metabolites • Primary route of excretion • Side effects	• Anatomy and physiology • Pharmacology • Disease management • Drug metabolism • Health outcomes • Patient profile • Conventional medical practice • Competitor products	• Sales review • Key product advocates • Product position and growth targets • Formulary status • Competitor activities • Healthcare structure • Healthcare expenditure and pricing

Figure 4.1: Three categories of essential knowledge

In early part of your sales career, you will need to focus on technical, medical and product knowledge. This will be complimented by acquiring market knowledge. Generally the technical knowledge will be easy to define and is unlikely to change as much as market knowledge.

When you are dealing with your customers, focus around their particular knowledge needs from your visit. You do not want to be caught out not knowing a pertinent fact about your product or company, which is publicly available information. Customers will need to be reassured through facts and data so that any factual doubt can be removed to support your product. Key areas of concern could include the following:-

- Prescribing rationale, including dosage, pack size etc
- Product interactions
- Safety profile
- Product availability
- Usage restrictions
- Price

Coach's Tip

You must be able to recall all key facts that come up frequently with your customers - your discussions will be enhanced if they are backed up with good facts and data

Competitive advantage

Knowledge is power as the old saying goes and it can be powerful to be able to relate facts and data which can differentiate you from your competitors. Experienced representatives will recognise that using your knowledge base is key to earning your right of entry into the customers' mind—even when the call may last mere 60-seconds.

Disease and product knowledge will help you to establish trust and credibility with healthcare professionals by meeting and exceeding their expectations. Ultimately, the goal of assessing success is to ensure customer readiness, which means being able to perform a sales call in the field at the right level and at the right time. The first step of customer readiness is to assess your disease and product knowledge. Pre—and post-quizzes can be used during the learning system to help you identify gaps in learning; final certification tests confirm knowledge acquisition to the required standard.

Assessments using a variety of techniques should be organised in stages to reflect the learning progression:

- Retention and recall of anatomy/physiology and product knowledge is assessed through various methods of testing, including written and computer tests as well as oral recall of facts
- Verbalising knowledge can be assessed using presentations or scripting
- Application of this knowledge to specific patient populations, for instance, can be assessed with interactive e-learning exercises or role-playing
- Integrating this learning into the sales-call model occurs in two steps:
  - Observing an experienced sales representative on a sales call.
  - Practicing sales calls using role-playing

The ultimate assessment will be a commercial one. The result of all this learning should be an increase in sales or market share. Having a sound knowledge base is a good starting point.

Learning styles

Learning styles varies, you may prefer written text to retain and assimilate knowledge and facts, or feel more comfortable with visual representations as the most effective way to learn. If you learn better through pictures or illustrations, try to summarise key points from a written text into series of simple diagrams that will help your understanding.

It is important to be aware of your learning preference and employ this in learning facts and data.

Ideally learning should be blended, which includes instructor-led activities and presentations, Web casts, role-playing workshops, self-study reviews and e-learning

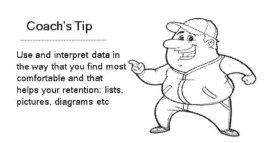

Coach's Tip

Use and interpret data in the way that you find most comfortable and that helps your retention: lists, pictures, diagrams etc

exercises, offers the range of learning options you will need. By anticipating different styles and approaches, blended learning enables you to align the delivery method with the type of content to: ensure that delivery matches your objectives, activate individual learning strengths and maximize engagement with content or activities.

Aligning delivery with the content means, for instance, using classroom time to build skills and apply theory. You should interact with your colleagues to articulate disease, product and clinical knowledge. Use the opportunity with role-playing to practice new techniques and behaviours. Group classroom sessions are too often wasted on basic-knowledge presentations that would be more effectively transmitted through Web casts or as personal reading assignments. One typical exception to this general practice is the common use of seasonal conventions to introduce new sales plans, marketing initiatives or recent studies and clinical results.

Information that is stable and infrequently revised, such as anatomy or physiology, is most suited to permanent publishing (in paper or digital form). Reading remains the most effective medium for independent study in any setting and an effective "story-telling" vehicle for typical therapeutic events.

E-learning can be an effective way to learn, especially for stable content and is ideally suited to building application and decision making capabilities. It's an ideal medium, for instance, for applying disease and product knowledge to identify applicable patient groups. It is important that these knowledge-based simulations are kept real through replicating your company's sales environment.

Using your knowledge effectively

It is helpful to understand some learning principles which should support what you have learnt effectively:-

- Use your experience in the field and apply newly acquired knowledge in the practical context, i.e. what is most important to your customers, what do they want to hear from you and how the new facts and data add value to your proposition (messages, arguments and discussion points)?
- You should bridge new learning to the existing personal knowledge base so that over the course of the promotion period it becomes routine
- Use whatever format that suits your individual learning style to learn and recall (summary notes, handwritten facts, mind maps etc)

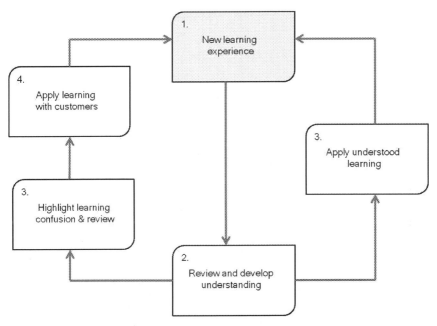

Figure 4.2: Learn, review and apply newly acquired knowledge

The key point to learning is to be able to apply in a practical way with your customers. Some facts and data will be easy to understand and digest, yet others will require more focus and attention so that it makes more sense. This will require review and discussion before it makes perfect sense (figure 4.2).

Field coaching can support your learning and development. This coaching should be consistent and rigorous so that the feedback you obtain demonstrates the changes that are implemented and the desired results from your customer activities are attained.

The role of your line manager in supporting your efforts will be important. He or she must be able to coordinate, where relevant with a field coach and have to ensure your newly acquired knowledge is effective in transferring changed behaviour in the field. Coaching should help to reinforce your learning.

It is important to evaluate the ongoing support and direction in learning that you are gaining from your line manager and field coach. Do not hesitate to seek additional help or clarification. Remember that the more clear your understanding, the more effective you become in your role and that will be to the mutual benefit to all concerned.

Your colleagues who may be promoting the same product range can be invaluable in helping your understanding and knowledge assimilation

---

Part four Summary

- You are the technical expert for your products and your credibility, in part, in front of the customer will depend on this
- Knowledge acquisition, retention and recall will give you a competitive edge
- Know your preferred learning style and use the mix of learning methods to aid your learning
- Use all the available resources in your company, including e-learning to develop your understanding
- Applying knowledge will depend on a mix of your experience, the context of the call or meeting and the relevance; use your judgement wisely

Part Five Team work

*The nice thing about teamwork is that you always have
others on your side*

Margaret Carty

*It is unlikely that you will be working in isolation and success very often
will depend on joint team efforts. Working effectively with colleagues
requires effort and energy but can ultimately affect your success. This
chapter looks at all aspects of teamwork.*

In most organisations, team work forms an important aspect of
commercial sales strategy. Teamwork can be expected at your
territory level where you share your work with another colleague,
your regional team, product team which can be at national level.

Approach to teamwork

Maintaining a very positive approach and attitude to working with
others will be important to achieve your desired outcomes. Just as
you work very hard to build customer relationships, likewise you
should also invest the time and energy to build the right rapport
and working relationship with all your internal colleagues, either
local or regional office based. Every individual in the team will bring
together some skill and aptitude that can be complimentary and
add to the richness of the team. Individuals will have their own
personality and ways of managing the required tasks.

Let us consider the areas where teamwork will be important and
the implications:

Territory teams

Often the required customer coverage and frequency can only be possible through a team of individuals who have shared targets, shared customers and shared geographical boundaries of responsibilities. Forming a strong partnership, mutual understanding and striving towards common goals will be important.

Regional teams

Your territory will be part of a regional structure in which your colleagues from neighbouring territories will be responsible for broadly a similar product portfolio. Quite often you will be working together in a cross functional structure or you may be involved in a joint project. It is important to share learning and ideas as well as gaining experience from others' territory and customer management approach.

Regional office teamwork

This can be part of an assignment with Marketing, Regulatory, HR etc. There will likely to be work for fixed duration and for specific purpose. Good communication will be essential especially if you are working remotely. You should seek clarity about your role if it is not clear as well as the desired outcomes you will be responsible for. There should be a clear leader who is responsible for overall coordination of the assignment.

Teamwork effectiveness

For any team to be truly effective, the ground rules must be clear, the understanding sound and support be available. Characteristically, there a number of attributes that you should pay particular attention to so that you are an effective team player and you also help others to reach the same heights (figure 5.1):

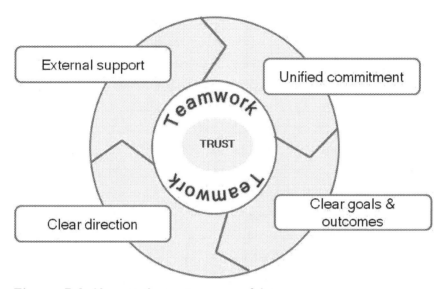

Figure 5.1: Key attributes in successful teams

- *Clear direction*: you and your colleagues should be fully clear on which way you are heading: right customers to see, how often, how you will divide responsibility, how you will communicate, how you will check progress etc.
- *Trust and collaboration*: create a climate in which there is open, honest and consistent behaviour by all team members. Reliability is an important ingredient and should be actively demonstrated. With this climate your team will perform well . . . without it, they can easily fail.

Coach's Tip

Really learn to embrace teamwork - don't just participate but actively contribute, it will get noticed

- *Clarity of goals and outcomes*: your team goals should call for a specific performance objective, expressed so concisely that everyone knows when the objective has been met. The direction must be clear, ideally with performance indicators and set time lines for individual and collective responsibility on all tasks.
- *Unified commitment*: This means that all team members must be directing their efforts towards the same goal. If your efforts are going purely towards personal goals, then the team's performance will be affected and members may confront this and resolve the problem.
- *External support*: a team can thrive when it has all the required resources and is well supported by line management. If you are in a position where this is lacking, you must raise the issue and get it addressed swiftly. Your teamwork must receive encouragement and support from your line manager as well other senior managers.

Building teamwork skills

Effective team working requires a number of basic skills which will help to ensure you and your colleagues work well together and have the right outcome. Figure 5.2 shows these four basic skills.

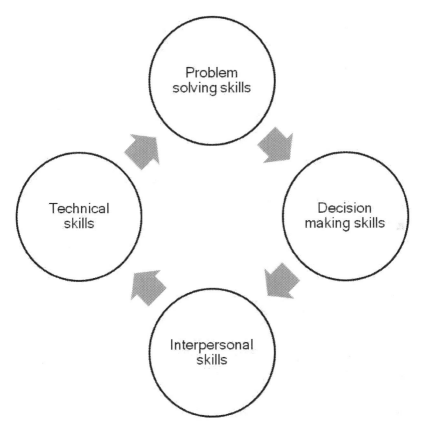

Figure 5.2: Essential skill set for working in teams

From this skill set, think around the any that you need further work on. Interpersonal skills are fundamental to all your efforts. Any member of your team that has difficulty getting along with others will cause disruption and can undermine all the good hard effort made by the rest.

Problem solving is an important asset to have. You need to think carefully about the problem or issue the team are facing assessing all possible angles, asking yourself some fundamental questions:

- What is the cause of the issue or problem?
- What are the possible outcomes?

- What is the overall objective that needs to be achieved?
- What improvements are required?
- What resources are available to solve issue or problem?
- What is the communication strategy?

Interpersonal skills are about your capacity to communicate ideas and thoughts in a professional way with the team. Different team members will view a specific issue in their own way and it is important that there is consensus on the final objective and interpretation of the road map that will lead to this outcome.

Technical skills refer to the knowledge and understanding of the team. Clearly, some team members will be more advanced or experienced and it is their role to bring others to the same level of understanding.

Finally, decision making is very important. The decision may be done collectively as group consensus or if you are elected as leader you may be asked to arrive at the decision taking into account all the available information.

Teamwork in perspective

Many territory teams are formed and will remain intact for a number of years. If you are in this situation, then enjoying the spirit of team work is invaluable. Figure 5.3 shows the classic progress of teams. It is important you can move swiftly from stage 2 (storming) and perform together at stage 4 (performing) quickly and consistently.

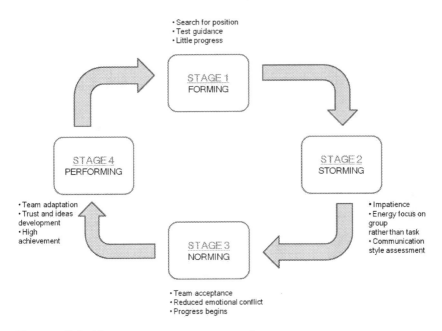

Figure 5.3: Key stages in team growth

Teamwork in the workplace does require a lot of care, sensitivity, and patience for it to pay off in the long run. This is not exactly the formula that most organizations run on these days. Typically we see organizations pre-occupied with putting out fires and handling crises. Most organizations have a very short-term focus and many leaders are not enlightened enough to invest in fire prevention and not get caught by the excitement of the task or by the activity trap that is so common today.

The problem we see in a lot of situations is that teamwork in the workplace is being killed by "friendly fire." In other words, we are directing our competitive energies

Coach's Tip

Learn from working with others as an aid to developing your skills in managing expectations and outcomes at looking better than another person or looking better than another team in the organization.

All too often we compete for personal rewards at the expense of others. We act as though our department is in a race with other departments, and we take our eye off the real competition.

Great achievements could be accomplished today if members and leaders trust and commit to the teamwork process of joint problem solving, consensus decision making and shared leadership and win/win conflict resolution.

Team conflict

This is something to watch out for in any teamwork that you are involved in. Conflict can arise from numerous sources within a team setting and generally falls into three categories: communication factors, structural factors and personal factors (figure 5.4)

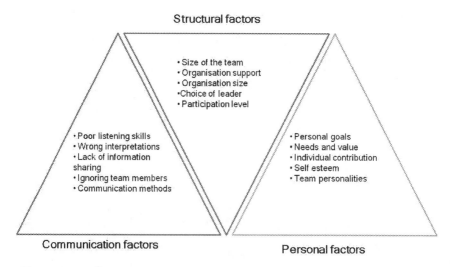

Figure 5.4: Team conflict categories

The first category is Communication: Poor listening skills, ignoring team members, wrongful interpretation and lack of sharing information are all a part of this barrier. These can lead to many misunderstandings. Any of these factors can cause strain in your progress with other team members. Make sure that your own communication is well thought out and professional, dealing with the key issues, specific on requests, clear on commitments and unambiguous in outcomes.

The second category is structural factors: the structure of the team and how this relates to the culture of your organisation is important. The choice of leader and your level of participation are very relevant and may affect your own or your colleagues outlook on the progress of the team.

Finally, personal factors: these include problems that can affect your self-esteem, the team personal goals, values and needs. All of these differences can pose a challenge for the team as a whole. It may be difficult to get everyone in the team working together and contributing equally.

Conflict does not always cause destruction. It can lead to a variety of ideas and give team members an interest in dealing with problems. It can provide an opportunity to develop your communication skills and express your personal thoughts to team members. If you look at it from this perspective, it can be considered a positive thing.

Conflict becomes negative when it is left to escalate to the point where you begin to feel defeated and a combative climate of distrust and suspicion develops. It is a good idea

Coach's Tip

Avoid personalising issues in a team - focus instead on the collective outcomes to keep your line manager informed around all aspects about your participation in all team activities, that way you can request support at an early stage so you avoid any frustration and get the required support.

There are some simple steps you can take to resolve team conflicts:

Identify team strengths and weaknesses

What will be one person's weakness will possibly be another team member's strength. It is important early on to have each team member identify for the group their skills. Team members should identify the areas in which they very effective and what areas they will be of least assistance. Some team members will be better at proof reading while others will be better at organizing and structuring the projects.

Recognise there will be different learning styles within the group. Your own style may be different from your colleagues: some team members will have good visual skills and they should be assigned visual task, such as creating tables, charts etc. A very important part of a team is having everyone contribute equally. If one person is given a higher workload then their teammates, conflict can develop. Team will need to lay out what is to be completed and from there distribute it equally to all members of the group.

Scheduling conflicts

People lead many different lives and have many different responsibilities, so it is not always easy for teams to coordinate a meeting. What is a good time for one member may be the busiest time of day for another. Thanks to modern technology, team meeting are easier to organise and implement. Use your internal meetings management tools, including message boards, chat rooms and regular teleconferences to keep connected on a regular basis.

Lack of equal participation

In order to support equal participation, your team needs to come together early and come to an agreement about participation levels. If participation is an issue there are several ways to go about resolving the lack of participation between members. Team members need to communicate with those they feel are not doing their part. It is possible that anyone who is not actively participating is not aware of how the group feels. Finding out what each member of the group is feeling is the best way to start before approaching a member who is not participating. If a group member does not want to give equal participation, the group needs to progress forward.

Understanding and overcoming differences

When you are addressing team conflict remember that the way in which it is handed is critical. You want to be able to manage any conflict in an effective manner so that you solve the problems but keep the group together at the same time. It would be of no advantage to the group if you chose the wrong approach to resolve conflicts and in turn break up the group. Teamwork is not something that can be demanded. It can be a fragile structure which needs to be handled delicately so as not to dissolve the group.

The key to successful group projects is encouragement of an open, frank dialogue among all participants. Once people feel as though they are able freely to express their viewpoints without undue criticism, a positive environment will develop. This kind of atmosphere is most conducive to productive work. At the same time, there should not be one individual that starts to dominate all team affairs.

After correctly identifying what specific problems have arisen in the group environment, the next step is eliminating these, to the extent possible. Think through several options which may work to differing degrees of success. The importance of appropriately classifying the difficulties the team is experiencing cannot be understated. Different problems may require fundamentally different responses.

Conflict Resolution

One method of conflict resolution is collaboration. After assessing each team member's ideas, the best parts are selected to form the whole. Cooperative efforts made by the team can produce good result. This system will be suitable for groups having delicate members and/or those with an inflated sense of self-worth. Perhaps the most effective method of conflict resolution is compromise.

The first—and possibly most-important part of compromising is the realisation that each person will have to relinquish something for the greater good. Once they can move beyond that, the rest is fairly simple.

While your colleagues may come up with certain measures of conflict resolution such as avoidance or accommodation, these can prove ineffective and may actually cause larger problems down the line. Walking away from the problem is not the right way.

Another method of solving disagreements is reassigning team members' role and responsibilities. By altering the construction, a more agreeable stance might be agreed upon. With different people assigned to new tasks, fresh ideas may emerge and the conflict may resolve of its own volition.

Disagreement amongst your group members does not necessarily have to represent a problem. In fact, a divergence of viewpoints can be celebrated as being a

Coach's Tip

In any team conflict, bring others back to the key business points and away from personality issues

valuable asset to the ultimate goal of the team. Groups, while sometimes born of necessity, may also be created specifically for the purpose of encouraging a more creative, diverse project through the input of several unique viewpoints.

Serious disagreement among team members can severely impact your work or even grind operations to a halt. Teams may try and prevent disruptions from even arising while working together, but inevitably, when people from different backgrounds with diverse viewpoints merge, there will be some measure of disagreement. In order for the team to be effective, a reasonable solution to conflicts needs to be understood and implemented.

Varying circumstances necessitate any one of a multitude of approaches. Where the level of disagreement cannot be resolved readily within the team you are working in, request help and support from your line manager or anyone senior who has an active interest in the outcomes from the team's progress. When the best process is applied, the problem can be discarded and the important work of the team can progress.

Part five Summary

- Teamwork is very often critical to your success, embrace it and enjoy working with others
- Effective teamwork is about building the trust, collaboration and the right support
- Think about which team building skills you need to focus upon and what type of support you need as well as identifying the right individuals
- Understand the causes of team conflict, which can stem from three key areas: communication, structure of the team and personal factors
- Take a proactive view of teamwork and aim to resolve any pending issues and conflicts at your earliest opportunity

Managing performance reviews

Success is the sum of small efforts, repeated day in and day out

Robert Collier

Performance reviews are essential to further your development and career. It is the formal opportunity to review your performance with your line manager and shape together your progress in your current role and beyond. Quite often performance review process can be daunting and seen as an 'unnecessary evil'. This chapter will focus on performance review as a tool that can help you develop and reach higher goals. By simplifying the approach and improving your understanding you can use the opportunity to your advantage.

Performance appraisal is an area where many sales professionals do not give their full attention and yet it is in most cases the document can further your career as well as affecting pay and benefits. Performance appraisals generally review your individual performance against objectives and standards for the year, agreed at the previous appraisal meeting. Many Managers and their sales teams commonly dislike appraisals and try to avoid them until the last moment or do a less than adequate job. To these people the appraisal is daunting and time-consuming. The process is seen as a difficult administrative chore and emotionally challenging. The annual appraisal is perhaps the only time since previous year that the two people have sat down together for a meaningful one-to-one discussion. No wonder then that appraisals are stressful—which then defeats the whole purpose.

Scope of performance appraisal

Your own organisation will have a systematic and sound appraisal performance system in place. You will need to ensure that you understand the whole process and are familiar with all components. Typically, performance documentation should capture all the essential elements that contribute to analysing your performance as well as your development:

- performance review—sales versus target achievements, key advocate development, new product launches etc
- clarifying, defining, redefining priorities and objectives
- motivation through agreeing helpful aims and targets
- motivation though achievement and feedback
- training needs and learning desires—assessment and agreement
- identification of personal strengths and direction—including unused hidden strengths
- career and succession planning—personal and organisational
- team contribution where appropriate
- personal and team training needs assessment and analysis
- reinforcing and cascading organisational philosophies, values, aims, strategies, priorities, etc
- delegation, additional responsibilities, your growth and development
- counselling and feedback

Coach's Tip

The performance review is an ideal opportunity to shine and not one to get anxious or concerned about

Increasingly there is less and less face-to-face time together these days. Performance appraisals offer a way to protect and manage these valuable face-to-face opportunities. You should hold on to and nurture these situations, and if you are under pressure to shorten any meaningful discussions and meetings, request another time or venue so that the process and outcomes are not compromised.

Performance appraisal process

Depending on the size and complexity of your organisation's commercial structure, the content of the appraisal process can range from few pages to a much lengthier document ten pages or more. In many companies, this process has become automated via an intranet facility and is rarely handwritten now. The traditional process has divided the process into three stages: annually and midyear but can be expanded to quarterly as well. Usually the year end annual performance appraisal is the key one, incorporating full year performance and sales data.

If your manager holds regular informal one-to-one review meetings, this will greatly reduce the pressure and time required for the annual formal appraisal meeting. The timing can be mutually agreed such as quarterly. There are several benefits of reviewing frequently and informally:

- The manager is better informed and more up-to-date with the team's activities (and more in touch with what lies beyond, e.g., customers, suppliers, competitors, markets, etc)
- Difficult issues can be identified, discussed and resolved quickly, before they become more serious

- Help can be given more readily—people rarely ask unless they see a good opportunity to do so—the regular informal review provides just this

- Assignments, tasks and objectives can be agreed completed and reviewed quickly—leaving actions more than a few weeks reduces completion rates significantly

- Objectives, direction, and purpose is more up-to-date—pace of change demands more flexibility than a single annual review allows—priorities often change through the year, so individuals need to be re-directed and re-focused

- Training and development actions can be broken down into smaller more digestible

Coach's Tip

If you have any doubts about the performance review process, talk to your manager *before* the event

chunks, increasing success rates and motivational effect as a result

- The 'fear factor', often associated by many with formal appraisals, is greatly reduced because people become more comfortable with the review process

- Relationships and mutual understanding develops more quickly with greater frequency between the line manager and the rep

- Much of the review has already been covered throughout the year so when the time comes for the formal appraisal, this should be an easy to manage meeting

- Frequent review meetings increase the reliability of notes and performance data, and reduce the chances of overlooking issues at the yearend appraisal

Maximise the opportunity

Performance appraisals require a systematic and organised approach. The extra effort and work that you put in will directly support your development. As a starting point, you should be clear what are the main components of the performance review, what is the format of the form that should be filled in and what are the timelines. Think of the whole process as a continuum aspect of your development and you can divide up the process into three areas to focus: performance in your role, business objectives and career dialogue (see figure 6.1).

Performance plan	Business objectives	Career dialogue
Key sales targets	Product market share	What do I see myself doing in the next 1-3 years?
Key performance areas to review	Key advocate relationships	What are the skills that I need to achieve these career aspirations?
Core non sales measures to focus on	Technical and product training needs	Is there anything that might hold me back from achieving my aspirations?

Figure 6.1: performance appraisal key areas of focus

Flow of performance appraisal

You can then take the following steps to ensure the process works well for you:

- **Prepare**—prepare all your notes records of performance, achievements, incidents, reports etc—anything related to performance and achievement. A good appraisal form will provide a good natural order for proceedings. If your organisation doesn't have a standard appraisal form then locate one. Whatever you use, ensure you have the necessary approval from your organisation, and understand how it works. Organise your paperwork to reflect the order of the appraisal and write down the sequence of items to be covered. If the appraisal form includes a self assessment section and/or feedback section (good ones do) ensure you have this suitably in advance of the appraisal with relevant guidance for completion. As part of your preparation you should also consider 'whole-person' development—beyond and outside of the job skill-set. You can balance your job skills training, and the required learning and development experiences. Very often an individual's natural talents and passions often contain significant overlaps with the attributes, behaviours and maturity that are required and valued in the workplace. Use your imagination in identifying these opportunities to encourage 'whole-person' development and you will find appraisals can become very positive and enjoyable activities. Appraisals are not just about job performance and job skills training. Appraisals should focus on helping the 'whole person' to grow and attain fulfilment.

- **Venue**—ensure a suitable venue is planned and available with your manager—free from interruptions—avoid hotel lobbies, public lounges, canteens—privacy is absolutely essential (it follows also that planes, trains and automobiles are entirely unsuitable venues for performance appraisals.)
- **Layout**—room layout and seating are important elements to prepare also—don't simply accept

whatever layout happens to exist in a borrowed or hired room—layout has a huge influence on atmosphere and mood—irrespective of content, the atmosphere and mood must be relaxed and informal—remove barriers—you must create a relaxed situation, preferably at a meeting table or in easy chairs—sit at an angle to each other, 90 degrees ideally—avoid face to face, it's confrontational.

- **Introduction**—go in with a relaxed mind-open with a positive statement, smile, be warm and friendly—it's your opportunity so being relaxed is very important. Your manager should explain what will happen—you should actively discuss all aspects related to your appraisal. Confirm the timings, especially finishing time. If helpful and appropriate begin with some general discussion about how things have been going, but avoid getting into specifics, which are covered next (and you can say so). Ask if there are any additional points to cover and note them down so as to include them when appropriate.

- **Review and measure**—review the activities, tasks, objectives and achievements one by one, keeping to distinct separate items one by one—avoid going off on tangents or vague unspecific views. If you've done your preparation correctly you will have an order to follow. If something off-subject comes up then note it down and commit to returning to it later (and ensure you do). Concentrate on hard facts and figures, solid evidence—avoid conjecture, anecdotal or non-specific opinions. Being objective may not be easy but is essential. Resist making quick judgments in your own mind, according to your own style and approach—facts and figures are the acid test and provide a good neutral basis for the discussion, free of bias and personal views. For each item agree a measure of competence or achievement as relevant, and according to whatever measure or scoring system is built into the appraisal system. This might be simply a yes or no, or it might be a percentage or a mark out of ten, or an A, B, C. Reliable review and measurement requires reliable data—if you don't have the reliable data you can't review and you might as well re-arrange the appraisal meeting. If a point of dispute arises, you must get the facts straightened out before making an important decision or judgement, and if necessary defer to a later date.

- **Agree an action plan**—An overall plan should be agreed with your manager, which should take account of the job responsibilities, your career aspirations, the departmental and whole organisation's priorities, and the reviewed strengths and weaknesses. The plan can be staged if necessary with short, medium and long term aspects, but importantly it must be agreed and realistic.

- **Agree specific objectives**—These are the specific actions and targets that together form the action plan. As with any delegated task or agreed objective these must adhere to the SMART rules—specific, measurable, agreed, realistic, and time-bound. If not, don't bother. The objectives can be anything that will benefit you and you will action upon.

- **Agree necessary support**—This is the support required for you to achieve the objectives, and can include training of various sorts (external courses and seminars, internal courses, coaching, mentoring, secondment, shadowing, distance-learning, reading, watching videos, attending meetings and workshops, workbooks, manuals and guides); anything relevant and helpful that will help the person develop towards the standard and agreed task. Also consider training and development that relates to 'whole-person development' outside of job skills. This might be a talent that you would like to develop. The best employers understand the value of helping the whole person to develop.

Easy way to manage the process

Being well organised and taking the performance management process into manageable chunks is the ideal way to prepare for both midyear and year end reviews.

The following factors should help you to stay focussed on the perfect outcome to every performance review you undertake:-

- Be prepared to discuss your annual objectives—think in terms of progress points and problem areas (areas where you are either unsure or have known weakness).

Coach's Tip

Spend some time and effort in completing your review documents - this will enhance your discussion meetings

- Check measurements for each objective. Are you staying focused on the higher priority objectives?
- Think about your non quantifiable measures such as behavioural objectives—the 1-3 you chose to work on for the year. How do you know you have made progress? What feedback have you had? This should be recorded on a regular (monthly or quarterly basis) in a suitable spreadsheet.

- What have you done to make progress on your Development Plan? What do you still need to do to continue your development? What questions do you have for your manager regarding your development?
- Think of ways your manager is helping you—and be prepared to say it. Think of ways your manager can guide you more effectively—and be prepared to say it. What is working for you? What is not?
- Did you do all of the preparation for the discussion? Now you are ready for the discussion. And one last suggestion: _Listen!_ Listen for suggestions from the manager. What do you need to Stop, Start, and continue doing?

Have a look at figure 6.2 which shows some typical questions to ask your line manager directly. Your development is important and should be included in your discussion at every opportunity. Stay focused on your performance over the past year—what you did well and how you did it, what you could do better. Take time to discuss the specifics of your Development Plan—after you and the manager have had time to reflect on your performance. Sometimes an annual review turns into a discussion of training programs, promotion possibilities, or new assignments—rather than the key purpose of the discussion—your performance over the past year.

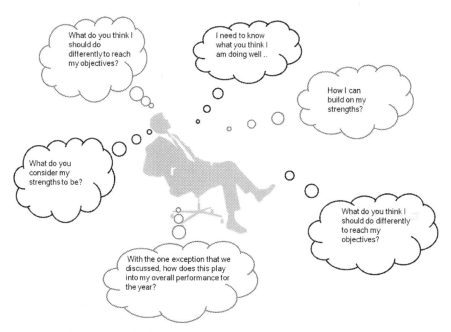

Figure 6.2: Some helpful questions to ask your line manager

Tips on completing the appraisal process

- Be as factual as you can be. Obviously if your manager does not have a positive and fair approach, be careful not to create vulnerabilities for yourself.
- Always be positive, never negative—don't complain, don't point out problems, avoid making personal attacks on anyone or their abilities. If there are problems express them as opportunities to develop or improve, an if possible suggest or recommend how these improvements can be made.
- Ask for help, training, coaching and development in those areas that you believe will improve your productivity and value to the company.
- Look for ways to relate personal growth and development of your own passions and interests outside of work, to

your work, and the benefits this sort of development will bring to your employer. Think about your hobbies and your natural strengths—they will almost certainly entail using many attributes that will be helpful for your employer—perhaps beyond the role that you find yourself in currently. If your company is unaware of your talents and potential make sure you tell your manager, and if your company fails to understand the benefits of helping you to follow your unique personal potential (which each of us has) then maybe think about finding another company that places a higher value on their people.

- Be specific, objective and be able to reference examples and evidence. This is an important area for the appraisal meeting itself so think about it and if necessary ask others for feedback to help you gather examples and form a reliable view of your competence in each category listed. If the appraisal form does not have a list of skills and behaviours create your own (use your job description as a basis).

- Assess your performance for the appraisal period (normally the past year) in each of your areas of responsibility (sales targets, customer relationships, coverage and frequency etc); if the specifics that are brought forward from the previous appraisal are unclear use your job description and Identify objectives for yourself for the next year. as a basis for assessing your performance, competence and achievements.

- Your objectives should be a mixture of short, medium and long-term aims (ie, days or weeks, months, and a year or more). Attach actions and measurable outputs to these aims and objectives—this is a commitment to change and improve which demonstrates a very responsible and mature attitude.

- If your aims and actions require training or coaching or other support then state this, but do not assume you have a right to receive it—these things cost money and your manager may not be able to commit to them without seeking higher approval.
- Think about and state your longer-term aspirations—qualifications and learning, career development, and your personal life fulfilment issues too—they are increasingly relevant to your work, and also to your value as an employee.
- Seek responsibility, work, projects and tasks within and beyond your normal sales role. Extra work and responsibility, and achieving higher things develop people and increase productivity for and contribution to the company.
- Always seek opportunities to help and support others, including your manager.
- Always look upon reward as an economic result of your productivity. You have no 'right' to reward or increase in reward, and reward is not driven by comparisons with what others receive. Reward and particularly increase in reward, results from effort and contribution to your performance. As such, if you want higher reward, seek first the opportunity to contribute more.

Ongoing Feedback

There are certain times when you should expect feedback on your work—after a large project is complete, during Mid-Year and Annual Reviews, during the Development Plan discussion—what about the rest of the time? Ongoing feedback can be an important part of your development. It provides an opportunity for you to know—in the moment—what you are doing well and what you need to improve. Ongoing feedback also gives you a chance to let your manager know what you need and expect from him/her—feedback works both ways.

Although it may sound a little artificial to some people, but honest, direct feedback—with the intention of helping someone to do the best work possible—is a gift. Receive feedback—and give it—with this positive intent.

Types of feedback

The type of feedback that you receive from your manager can generally be broken down into two key areas:

Motivational: this relates to areas that you have done particularly well on and you both share together the success. This need not be a major or spectacular event or a project; it could be simple as winning over a difficult customer or an improvement in call delivery etc.

Developmental: this is about behaviour or skills in need of improvement. This can be specific relating to a specific incidence or occurrence or can be general. In either case you should seek clarity from your manager if you are unsure or the feedback cannot be substantiated to any degree. In most cases there should be only one or two areas to be highlighted. The key is to have an action plan at the end of this feedback session.

Here are some ways you can look at giving and receiving feedback:

- **Receiving feedback.** Talking to your manager about your performance on a regular basis helps you stay on track—or get back on track. It is easier to make a simple shift in behaviour or an action—if

Coach's Tip

Take feedback in the right spirit - as a developmental opportunity and use it to push yourself toward achieving your goals

  you have not established a pattern. OR—it is a lot easier to establish a pattern if you know what is working. This feedback will help you become aware of areas that need improvement, skills/capabilities that are progressing and current areas of proficiency. Ask your manager to cite specific examples when giving feedback and to provide helpful suggestions for improvement.
- **Giving feedback.** The purpose of giving feedback is to provide suggestions and comments, in a constructive way, about specific examples—not general observations or impressions. When asked to give feedback to a team member or your manager, remember to give specific examples such as "Your ability to listen to all views and drive the decision making process on project X was beneficial to moving the project forward" or "I did not receive enough direction from you on project X as we were getting started; I would really appreciate a little more detail on the next one".
- **Input from others.** You do not have to wait for your manager to give you feedback. Sitting down with a colleague or dotted-line manager can be just as helpful in your development. Ask someone that you trust to be

honest, direct and helpful. You can talk about how a specific project is going, about your objectives for the year or whether or not the person has observed improvement in a specific skill you have been developing.

- **Next steps.** It is important to listen to the constructive feedback you have been given and take action on it. If you receive positive comments, great! Continue to do what you have done and look for ways to build upon this strength. If the feedback you receive is negative, ask for suggestions on how to improve—how to do it differently next time. Take action and make it part of your development process.

Part six Summary

- Performance appraisal is a good opportunity for you to showcase your achievements, re-calibrate to the sales strategy and adjust the direction you are heading towards
- Take time and make the effort to manage your performance review in a highly organised and professional manner
- Spend time before the review and add as much detail as possible so that the discussion and review is meaningful both for you and your line manager
- Receiving regular and consistent feedback is invaluable and will aid your review process
- Do listen to the feedback you get from your line manager, discuss any areas for clarification and commit to action

Part Seven Career development

If you wish to achieve worthwhile things in your personal and career life, you must become a worthwhile person in your own self-development

Brian Tracey

Career management is a critical component of your development. Like all endeavours, it requires focus and attention and cannot happen accidently. It is important that at every stage of your development in your sales role you have full visibility on the future direction that you want to aspire to, the steps that will help you get there and you have all the required support around you. This chapter will give you guidance and direction upon which you will be able to make sound decisions that will affect your career.

Many senior managers, business leaders and CEOs started their career as sales representatives. These individuals have discovered the value of understanding the entire business model focussed on the needs of their customers as well as being able to link together sales and marketing strategy, benefit of compliance and regulations and thorough understanding of the dynamics and significance of the sales role to a healthcare company.

In the past working in the private sector meant a certain degree of security with regular pay increments and a clear promotion plan. Most companies developed their own managers from regular intake of trainees; it was common to find senior managers and board members with 20-40 years of service. Careers blossomed through senior managers trained to recognise junior talent and nurture it. Junior staff also had to 'prove' their worthiness through number of years spent within a particular role or job category.

Today the pace of change and business dynamics means that the degree of uncertainty is high for sales professionals working within healthcare. Added to this is that fact that many individuals do not know exactly what career path they should follow and drift through a series of roles. The individuals may be talented, flexible or just lucky with the right circumstances, which can mean either having a good career, missing out on opportunities or never finding the right choices to make.

Critical success factor

The key question to ask yourself is 'are you enjoying your role?' The answer to this question will determine the motivating factors that affect your career aspirations and development. We do see some sales professionals who do not seem happy with their work and as a result are often looking for a job. Of course, there may well be some valid underlying sound reasons for dissatisfaction. In general these can be classified into the following areas:

- *Work itself*—seeing customers and developing your territory, which should be highly motivating
- *Responsibility*—meeting your activity and sales targets
- Achievement—joy of achieving market share growth and sales targets exceeding
- *Recognition*—hitting targets and gaining your bonus
- *Interpersonal relations*—getting on well with management and colleagues
- *Company policy and admin work*—far too much paperwork and or approvals in the system
- *Advancement*—seeing promotion opportunities open up

As you can see from this list, career advancement is just one of many areas of concern to most sales professionals and how quickly and effectively you advance will also depend on the factors above as well as being with the right company, in the right business environment (growth phase for your products) and having the right connections.

Career options

Before we explore some career paths within commercial setting, it is helpful to ask yourself what really excites you: do you enjoy field based work and prefer customer interface roles or an office based role that is internally focussed? Are you creative and like developing plans and ideas or do you find fulfilment in analytical oriented tasks?

The sales representative position is an ideal platform to develop and grow your future career. Acquiring the following skills will be important factors to pursue career advancement:

- Understanding customer needs

Coach's Tip

Which direction, sales or marketing? In the very best organisations, these functions work very closely together so you can change direction later

- Market knowledge, healthcare infrastructure and policies
- Key advocates and market opinion leader relationships
- Therapy and product knowledge
- Proven track record of success in field sales

Simply demonstrating the above factors is, of course, neither an entitlement nor a guarantee of successful career advancement.

Before commencing further discussion around preparation and readiness, it will be helpful to review some of the main career options that are available to you in most healthcare companies.

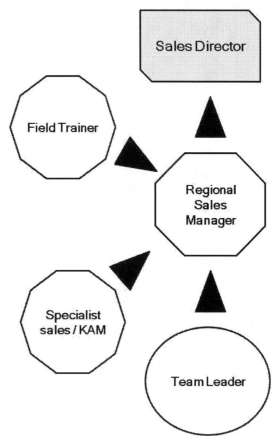

Figure 7 1: Sales career options

Sales

For many sales reps, the continuity into a management role in sales is a natural career path that is very well defined with clear roles and responsibilities. If your goal is to be a Sales Director, then the first step to sales management path has to be your main objective. This role can be a Regional Sales Manager where you have full responsibility for a single or multiple product teams with a defined geographical responsibility. Depending on your experience in your current role, you may want to consider a hybrid role (if this option is available to you) such as a Team Leader where you have partial management responsibility, usually over a small group, as well as sales responsibility over your own territory. This can be a less risky option or a stop gap measure to full sales management. The Field Trainer role can be fulfilling especially if you enjoy assisting and supporting your colleagues with their customer calling. This option can give you a better understanding of customer interactions and this experience will be invaluable to managing a team of representatives in the future.

One key task for a regional sales manager is to manage, motivate, coach and develop the sales representatives. Typically you could have anywhere from eight to fifteen representatives under your leadership. There will be some team diversity and experience. A major part of your week will be spent in field work with your representatives where you accompany them in their sales calls, observing how they interact with their customers. After the sales call you provide guidance and feedback on ways to improve. As a regional sales manager you will also be involved in sales forecasting, objective setting and budget management for your region and its territories. Planning regional meetings and organizing all the logistics will be a regular task, as well as working with the marketing department on marketing strategies and tactics to help improve sales. As with any management position, there is a large amount of administrative work that can include anything from data analysis to completing and approving expense reports to head office reports. In addition, a key responsibility is to work closely with your specialist representatives to help them develop some of the top key opinion leaders in your region to become advocates for your products.

To successfully obtain a position as a regional or district sales manager, you need to have proven success in field sales and in some cases progressive positions within the sales structure. Proven leadership skills are an absolute must for this type of position and if you do not prove yourself early in your career it will be difficult for you to obtain this level of position. As a manager, you will make decisions on a daily basis, so the ability to analyse information and make decisions quickly is a necessary skill to develop. Showing strong initiative and being action oriented are also critical to success. Finally, you will have needed to demonstrate that you are a strong team player in all aspects of the business to be considered for this position.

The pinnacle of field sales management is the National Sales Manager or Sales Director role. Once you are at this level, you have proven that you can lead a team, make good decisions, and have a very thorough understanding of how to grow the business.

National sales management involves managing, training and development of your direct reports. At this level of management it is the divisional sales managers who you work closely with. Strategy development is a significant part of this position, not only for sales and marketing, but working with the executive team to develop the overall corporate strategy. As with other management positions, sales forecasting, objective setting, meeting organization and planning are all important aspects to master. The team will look for you to set the vision for the organisation.

To be eligible for a national sales management position, you must demonstrate three to five years of successful divisional sales management and a clear focus on the big picture from a corporate perspective. In these positions the successful candidates are typically being groomed for VP or higher positions. Leading by example is an absolute necessity to obtain this position.

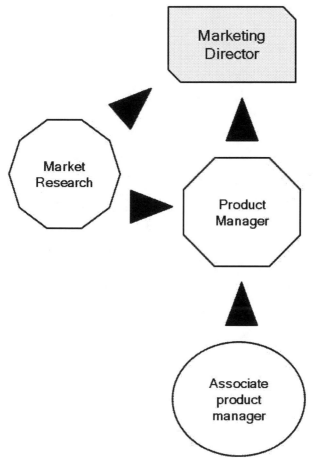

Figure 7 2: Marketing career options

Marketing

For many this is the preferred career choice with product management role carrying a high status amongst representatives in the field. There will be limited number of positions available compared to field sales and therefore, can be more competitive to gain.

The Marketing department develop materials for product launches and organise conferences and exhibitions. It is also be responsible for advertising; websites; the company intranet; newsletters; direct mailers; market research, analysis and intelligence; and forecasts for the product life cycle. Importantly, it is the Marketing department who will work with other Managers to develop the selling materials that the Sales Representatives use. Your experience in the field will be invaluable in your quest for a marketing role.

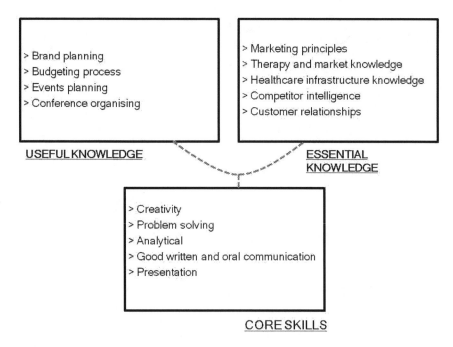

Figure 7.3: Marketing role criteria assessment

Figure 7.3 shows the core skills that are needed with some aspects of useful and essential knowledge that would support your application. This should give you a sound platform upon which to pursue a Marketing career.

Product managers (PM) are involved in budgeting, market research and strategic planning for either one product or a group of products within a therapeutic area. If you are an associate PM, PM or Group PM, your position will determine how far ahead you have to plan when thinking of the marketing strategy for your product or products. In product management you are responsible for creating all of the sales and marketing tools which representatives use on territory. Tools such as detail aids, dose cards, product advertisements and anything else used by a field sales representative to sell the products are created by you with the assistance of ad agencies. You are given a budget which you must allocate to support national and international congresses and conferences. It is your responsibility to analyze all of the options and determine which provides the best ROI and long term strategic impact. Product managers also work closely with the training managers in the development of training materials. If you are at a product manager level or above, you will also need to manage the people below you, so leadership must be proven early to obtain a PM position and advance within the department.

Your relationship with your current marketing team will be invaluable in gaining useful background information and appreciation of the product manager's role. Your insight should be able to reveal the nature of the role as well as the demands and pressures that go with it.

Like sales management roles, you may have two further options that can give you entry into Marketing: Associate Product Manager and Market Research Coordinator. The latter can be an analytical role in which you help and support business functions through both primary and secondary data provision.

You should consider an additional Marketing qualification such as the CIM (Chartered Institute of Marketing) Diploma in Marketing (UK) which can give you a valuable insight into marketing principles as well theory and practice. This will prove helpful when you make a formal application or when you want to discuss marketing roles in your organisation as it demonstrates serious intent. Combining part time study with your work commitments can be a little challenging but certainly achievable providing you plan well, set clear outcomes and objectives in mind and practice disciplined learning habits.

Sales Training Managers

As a sales training manager you have a great opportunity to demonstrate your field sales skills and experience. Transforming a representative into a more knowledgeable and effective sales person is a great challenge. Using your ability to take complex therapeutic and product information and break it down into simpler terms will help you teach all company employees effectively.

Within the training department you may start out as a field training manager for a particular geographic area. In this type of position you work closely with regional managers to develop regional or divisional representatives. You can then progress into a head office training role where you handle training for all company products, or just one particular therapeutic area, depending to on the size of the company.

After mastering the training managers position, you could be promoted into a Director (or VP) of Training and Development role. As you can see, even within the training department there are several opportunities for advancement. Training is typically seen as a developmental position for higher positions, so doing a great job will help you develop the skills to further advance your career into other areas.

As a Field Training Manager you will be more involved in the field coaching of representatives on their territory where you will observe their sales calls to provide feedback on improvement areas and reinforce their positive skills. If you are a head office trainer, you will primarily be involved in creating and organising head office training sessions. Also, all training managers are responsible for assisting sales representatives on all aspects of skills training. Researching the correct answer and providing it to the field representatives is a very common responsibility of a training manager.

To become a training manager you must prove yourself as a successful representative and show a high aptitude for technical information. Not only do you need to be able to understand detailed information, but you must also have the ability to clearly present it in a variety of ways. As each representative or manager learns differently, you must be able to adjust your teaching style to match their learning style. As training is considered a development role for higher positions, you must be a proven leader and team player in your sales roles. Overall, excellent presentation, organisation and time management skills are necessary and you must be very comfortable presenting to groups, both large and small. You must enjoy interacting with and helping your colleagues. The passion and desire to excel in the field are prerequisites.

Coach's Tip

Sales training can offer a great interim option and give you valuable experience with the sales force as well and develop relationships further

Government Affairs Manager

The governmental affairs position is an extremely important position. Most healthcare companies have to deal with governmental regulation and this role formally provides your company's interface with the government.

In this position, you work closely with the government and possible private insurance companies to gain formulary approvals for your products. This is important to gain reimbursement from the government or private insurance company. In order to do this, you would present clinical data to government officials and medical consultants who work with the government, to ensure any questions about the products are answered. In addition, this role involves a fair amount of negotiation with health agencies in an attempt to create a win-win-win situation for the government, the patients, and the pharmaceutical company.

These are very senior level positions and typically involve people who have at least five to ten years of sales management or director level experience and possess excellent negotiation and political skills. To be most successful, you need to have tremendous versatility in your sales style as you must handle both PR (public relations) and clinical presentation duties equally well.

Overall, no matter what position in a company you hold, it is very important at all times to represent your company and your industry in the most professional and respectful manner, according to both company and industry guidelines. You must learn to treat your territory as your own business and ensure that any funds you spend generate as high a return on investment as possible. If you treat your job as if you were running your own business and use your resources (both financial and time) to ensure a maximum return on investment, you will succeed. In addition, ensure you treat all customers (not just key ones) with respect ... that includes internal and external customers.

Other roles

If you have particular interest in HR, finance or logistics, these areas can be explored. The exact nature and definition of role and responsibilities will vary but in general these disciplines will require a degree of specialisation that is probably best met at an early stage in your career development. All three will require further qualifications and many years of experience to reach a senior level.

Take the opportunity and speak with respective directors and managers in the function you are most interested in and enquire as to what are the key requirements:

- What is an ideal starting role?
- How is the grading structure different from purely commercial roles?
- What is the entry qualifications and what additional qualifications or study will be needed?
- What career paths and options will be open to you in the future?
- What are the main challenges in the chosen function and how will this change in the future?
- What are the key attributes that will be looked for and what can you do to improve your chances of success?

Remember to speak to your line manager and seek the needed support, linking into performance appraisal and the annual career dialogue—the clearer the destiny in your own mind, the clearer you will be able to communicate this to your manager.

Take the opportunity and speak to relevant people who are currently in that role you desire. Ask them about their experience, what the role is really like and what are their challenges. You can take this one step further and discuss any relevant project that you can take part in which will give you a much better insight as well as raising your profile for upcoming positions.

Self analysis

Having discussed some career options, it is important that you pay attention to understanding yourself better as a starting point towards any current and future career options. Self evaluation is never an easy exercise, it takes some discipline to ask yourself some searching questions and commit to answering these as objectively as you can. Being honest with yourself is critically important. Seeking feedback from your colleagues is important. This feedback should be taken within the right context and more importantly, the feedback must be acted upon with immediate effect. Don't fall into the habit of either dismissing this feedback or limiting it to particular individuals and their habits. Concentrate on the actions that you can develop and the changes you can make which will enhance your career prospects.

Times are tough even in the world of healthcare sales. Being average or mediocre will no longer be sufficient. Many companies have recently gone through at least a few waves of redundancies and cut backs. One thing is for sure, you must remain proactive with your career management if you wish to remain somewhat in control of your destiny.

That being said, approach to career management need not be a complex exercise. It starts with critical self analysis. Figure 6.4 shows an example of the questions that you should focus on. By answering these points effectively, you will be in a much better position to pursue your ambition. Have a balanced approach to looking at your motives, activities, communication and performance and use this as the basis upon which you can:-

- Effectively evaluate the direction and focus you currently have
- Address the development areas to enhance your prospects
- Grow and develop as an individual

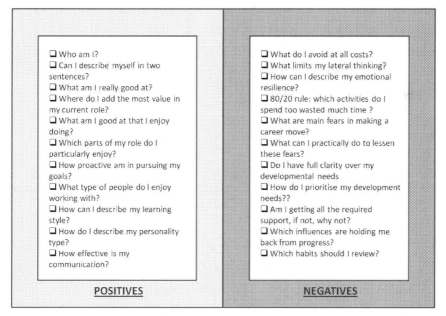

POSITIVES	NEGATIVES
❏ Who am I? ❏ Can I describe myself in two sentences? ❏ What am I really good at? ❏ Where do I add the most value in my current role? ❏ What am I good at that I enjoy doing? ❏ Which parts of my role do I particularly enjoy? ❏ How proactive am in pursuing my goals? ❏ What type of people do I enjoy working with? ❏ How can I describe my learning style? ❏ How do I describe my personality type? ❏ How effective is my communication?	❏ What do I avoid at all costs? ❏ What limits my lateral thinking? ❏ How can I describe my emotional resilience? ❏ 80/20 rule: which activities do I spend too wasted much time ? ❏ What are main fears in making a career move? ❏ What can I practically do to lessen these fears? ❏ Do I have full clarity over my developmental needs ❏ How do I prioritise my development needs?? ❏ Am I getting all the required support, if not, why not? ❏ Which influences are holding me back from progress? ❏ Which habits should I review?

Figure 7.4: Critical self evaluation

Once you have taken a self analysis, it is useful to link this with a clear direction and focus. To further assess your readiness and sense of direction, appendix 1 is a flow diagram that can help you to answer some key questions to check if you are clear on your outlook and direction. What is important to note is that if at any stage you feel unsure of your career direction, you must go back and keep asking the right questions and examine your focus and approach to making the ideal career move. This repetitive process will help you think clearly and take a step back and reflect on the choices you have made.

Find a label for yourself

Once you have full clarity of your interests, have a better understanding of your skills and abilities, it is useful to put all of this into a concise form: *create an ideal label for yourself*. This label will be carefully crafted by you to fit the needs of your next career move.

Ideally you should find elements which go to the core of you or which is unusual in some way. It should be simple and need not be overly complicated. Examples can include:-

- A hardworking and reliable individual . . .
- Highly motivated and dedicated sales representative . . .
- A multilingual, successful sales professional . . .

This statement now should be followed by skills or abilities or maybe a description of the role sought depending on your context. This 'label' will now appear on your CV, in letters and in conversation both formal and informal.

So from the above examples we can develop these further as follows:

- A hardworking and reliable individual, active team player and quick learner with capacity to focus on outcomes.

Coach's Tip

Research the dept (internal) or company (external). This will add real value to your discussions and interviews.

- Highly motivated and dedicated sales representative with outstanding communication and organisational skill.
- A multilingual, successful sales professional with strategic and business planning skills.

Role search tools

Whether you are applying for an internal vacancy or external one, the basic requirements of a CV, interview, assessment centres etc will be similar. Of course, the level of detail and emphasis will vary from internal to external. You may be fortunate to be offered a role purely on the basis of your CV and exceptional performance but in most circumstances a CV followed by interview or discussion would be normal.

Purpose of a CV

There are two key purposes that your CV should serve:

- Promote yourself for the potential and applied role
- Enable you to supply selected, factual and useful data about you

What you decide to include in your CV is important. The essential elements in every CV include:

- Details about yourself and how to contact you—include secure email address as well as home address and relevant contact number
- What are your skills and abilities—very straightforward language to express what you are good at, not necessarily how good you are at it—judgement must be left to others
- Your achievement to date—include any previous employment as well as the current role—this is crucial evidence to reassure the reader and support your skills and abilities
- Educational and qualification background—include all the essentials but avoid excess details, particularly if you have been in your current role for a while after the qualifications were gained
- Some personal information—you can share your interests and hobbies

Constructing a CV

It is important that your CV is well laid out, clear and direct to the point. It is worth paying attention to content as well as layout. The CV should be neatly styled and should be visually appealing as this will create the right first impression to someone who does not know you well.

The level of detail is important. Whether you are applying for an internal position or external one, laying out your performance succinctly and to the point is important. If you have undertaken many tasks and projects, there will be the temptation to include all of it; resist this and focus on tasks and projects that can demonstrate both outcome and more importantly *your individual contribution that added value.*

Depending on the position you want to apply for, your CV may not be read very closely. This will especially be true if you apply for an open position with many applicants or to an external company. In such circumstances where there can be more than 100 CVs to go through, recruiters will be looking to reduce such a number by rejecting, and almost any reason may suffice: too long, difficult to understand, missing information or something negative.

It is important that your CV describes you, as you believe yourself on your best days. You need to feel totally comfortable with the content and you can defend any sentence in it.

Finally remember that your communication starts with your written CV. You should make it clear and easy for the reader to go through all the details:

- Clear headings
- Sufficient white space around headings and sections
- Minimum number of different type faces and styles

Parts of the CV

1. Objective: this is optional, but may be useful to specify the type of role and company you seek and your intended contribution
2. Profile: description of you, little background information, and what you can offer an organisation in terms of strengths and experience

3. <u>Career highlights and selected achievements</u>: this is optional but around 4 or 5 notable achievements (merit awards, contribution and projects etc) can be useful

4. <u>Career</u> details: essential component, a list in reverse order of positions you have held with dates, demonstrating your achievements or contributions you have made—should be kept very succinct and to the point with clear outcomes highlighted

5. <u>Education and training</u>: in reverse order, starting with your highest qualification

6. <u>Personal details</u>: date of birth, key interests etc.

Your CV should be printed, easy to read, brief and to the point (one to three pages), positive and reassuring

---

You can use the myriad of templates and online tools that are available if this helps or alternatively simply construct your own from scratch. Have a look at examples of well constructed CVs provided at the

Coach's Tip

Most CVs are submitted via email these days, but if you want to send by post, print on high quality white or cream paper... use a clear and easy font.

end of this chapter. Once you have a CV you are fully satisfied with, updating should be straightforward.

Accompany your CV

A well written letter or email to accompany your CV is essential. The purpose is to put the CV into context and briefly give a couple of reasons for applying but it must not simply duplicate contents of your CV but to enhance its appeal and improve your chances. Use simple, short sentences to get your message across, write:

- An opening paragraph that immediately shows your relevance and makes a connection between you and the role you want
- Highlights of your relevant strengths or achievements
- Strong concluding paragraph that either requests a meeting or looks forward to an arranged meeting

Interview techniques

Following any written communication and your CV submission, in most cases you will be required to attend a formal interview. Being a little nervous before the interview is quite normal and may help you to be focussed and alert for the interview.

Some individuals will do well in interviews and most companies may not take too much account of the interview technique, good or bad. This may also be applicable to the interviewer. In any case the quality of communication is important so you should pay attention to your overall performance.

Use your label

Earlier we discussed having a label that you can use to help describe yourself for constructing your CV. You can extend this concept for the interview and create an advert for yourself which should be a mixture of the following:-

- Your key strengths (those that are relevant to the job you are applying for)
- Brief background information

- One or two career achievements or highlights

This will help you with the opening of the interview when you may be particularly nervous but as this is early in the interview process, keep it short and you can finish by offering to expand on any area. Have a look at the two examples below, you should get an idea of the sort of information that you have to give as well as the speaking style which will help to ensure you come across very natural and precise.

Coach's Tip

Keep letters of reference, sales awards, good performance reviews and other material that document your success...can be invaluable during your discussions

Example 1
I think I am creative, usually good at discovering non standard ways of approaching my work but at the same time I do think logically and analytically. One of my recent projects, which received internal company recognition, involved ways of engaging customers into treatment options for their patients with optimal outcomes that were particularly appreciated by key advocates.

Example 2
I have always been an effective communicator and particularly enjoy meeting people from diverse backgrounds. This outlook has helped me design a Marketing campaign which helps to address the needs of consumers in the Far East and Western markets. I particularly enjoyed training people in small groups in respect to this campaign.

Interview components
The interview is a two way process: for the manager to decide if you are suitable and for you to confirm this is the position you want and the manager will be right for you. Undoubtedly content of the

interview is more important than getting the right style. The interview can be broken down into following components:-

- Thoughts, ideas, opinions about the job and company, the market place, yourself and your career etc
- Factual discussions including statements about abilities, skills and experience
- Expressions and attitude: enthusiasm, curiosity, optimism, confidence etc

Coach's Tip

'How do you deal with missing targets?' sum up your answer with analytical response and share your learning

If the CV and accompanying letter or application form have already expressed your ideas and feelings about the job and facts about you, the interview will be easier.

Certain questions can be predictable and obvious. Take some time to reflect on such questions (example shown in figure 6.5). Being well prepared will ensure you can approach such questions with a deal of confidence.

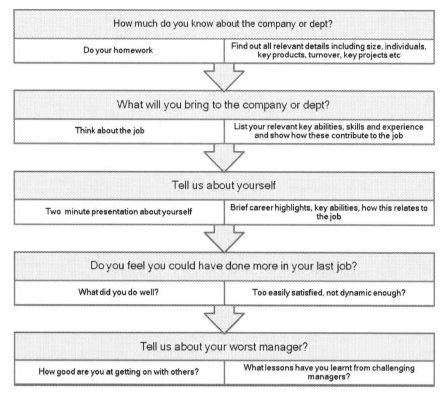

How much do you know about the company or dept?	
Do your homework	Find out all relevant details including size, individuals, key products, turnover, key projects etc

What will you bring to the company or dept?	
Think about the job	List your relevant key abilities, skills and experience and show how these contribute to the job

Tell us about yourself	
Two minute presentation about yourself	Brief career highlights, key abilities, how this relates to the job

Do you feel you could have done more in your last job?	
What did you do well?	Too easily satisfied, not dynamic enough?

Tell us about your worst manager?	
How good are you at getting on with others?	What lessons have you learnt from challenging managers?

Figure 7.5: Examples of frequent and sensitive questions

Any questions for us?

At the end of the interview you will have the opportunity to ask meaningful questions. Do not waste this opportunity. As well as clarifying any specific issues related to the recruitment process, it is

Coach's Tip

Before the interview, imagine yourself being professional, interesting and enthusiastic and this good feeling should put you in a positive frame of mind

worth asking a strategic question that relates to the department or company. You can also ask the interviewer what he likes particularly about the company.

Assessment centres

Following a formal interview you may be asked to attend an assessment centre. This is an opportunity for you to showcase your abilities and aptitude and for hiring managers to further distinguish between a number of candidates. Depending on your organisation and the role that you are applying for, any of the following may be included as part of the assessment:

1. *Psychometric tests*

Many large organisations use tests as a way of working out whether or not a candidate has the knowledge, skills and personality for a particular role. These psychometric tests can help identify individuals who may be suitable for future leadership positions.

Figure 6.6 shows four key areas that can be included in a typical test.

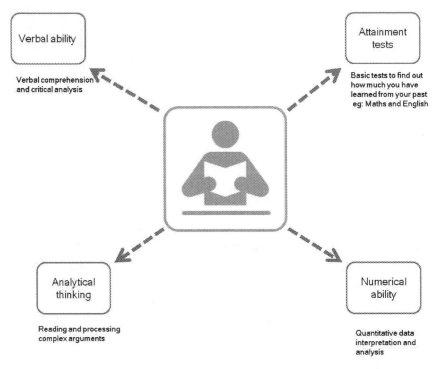

Figure 7.6: Key areas for psychometric testing

Irrespective of the type and form of tests, good preparation will be essential. Being well rested and in good physical shape can help. For personality and career aptitude tests, knowing yourself, your career and aspirations is the key. Do spend time thinking about your life and career goals. Do follow the common sense approach:

- Firstly, go through the whole test, answer questions you are absolutely sure about
- Go back over those questions and tackle those that you are confident about
- If you still have time left, go through remaining questions once again, really think them through, and provide your best answer

2. Group exercises

Leadership, teamwork and interpersonal skills are being assessed in any group exercise. Your ability to participate and contribute to a set exercise is important. There has to be a right balance of quantity and quality. From an invigilator's perspective such exercises can be often chaotic and disorganised. You should not worry about that but what you say and how you come across will be noted. The following general points should help:

- Learn as many names as you can so that you can refer to individuals more professionally

Coach's Tip

Do ask for feedback after a test, usually the HR dept will have this responsibility

- At any juncture where a summary is helpful or where the direction of discussion is unclear take the opportunity to direct the team
- Use the available facts and data to make a recommendation. Make it clear and precise with a succinct explanation. If the area under discussion is very familiar to you, express this fact but only if this add real value to the ongoing dialogue
- Be careful to display the right visual expressions as well as the language you use
- There may be individuals who want to 'demonstrate' their leadership by hijacking the discussion and interjecting at every opportunity. This type of individual should be meaningfully challenged with an appropriate question or request

- Clarity of response, coherent arguments and logical thought process are all important. Make brief written notes of the key points of the discussion and your own contribution and in your verbal response mention you have made some useful notes that help with the discussion
- Finally, remember there may not be a right or wrong answer but how you respond on the day will set you apart

3. Individual presentations

There will be a set time limit to prepare and deliver your presentation. Make careful note so that you can use the available time wisely. If you are given a choice of topics, select one that you have more familiarity and content that you feel most comfortable with.

Preparation

- Decide how many slides you will require in the available time with an estimate of how long each slide will take
- Make your theme and discussion very clear and precise; must have logical flow
- Try to avoid using more than five bullet points on each slide
- Illustrations, diagrams and pictures must be relevant, it is probably unlikely that you will have so much time to conduct intensive research, and it will not be necessary as the key objective will be *how well you prepare within time and resource constraints*, just like real business life
- Visual creativity in terms of slide transitions, sound effects and animation must be kept very professional

so that this does not distract from the content and discussion—stick to neutral colours and backgrounds

Delivery

- Don't forget all the basics of a good presentation: clear voice, good visual contact and precise response to all questions
- Give a brief explanation of what you have selected and why as well as how this contributes to the value of the presentation
- If you asked to make an opinion or take sides in a discussion, give a concise and clear explanation. Avoid taking too much time on an individual point of discussion as this will not demonstrate balance thought expressions

4. *Structured interviews*

Much of the general interview advice will still be applicable. The key difference is that structured interviews will require more specific response to a series of interview questions that can be either isolated or linked together. In particular you can be asked about a specific situation or an example from your experience which help to show how your actions added value.

Choose a clear and specific example that can best show your individual contribution. Figure 7.7 shows a structured way of approaching each example. By following the 'STAR' formula you will ensure that the required information is given with clear emphasis on your own contribution that made the difference to the outcome.

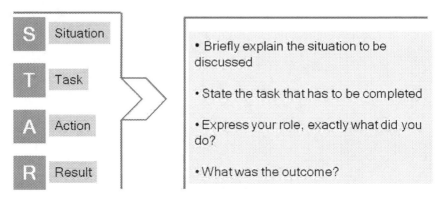

Figure 7.7: systematic way of approaching a structured interview

Take your time with selecting the examples that show you in the best light. Break them down into some inevitable categories such as teamwork, customer management and rising to a challenge. Highlight the importance of the issue to the company, what was required, what you did to make the difference and the final result of your endeavours.

5. In tray exercises

This is a business simulation, where you will be requested to play a member of staff who has to deal with the tasks of a busy day. You will be given a selection of letters; emails and reports in either paper or electronic format, which somebody doing the job might find in their in-tray or email inbox first thing in the morning.

You should read each item, decide on the action to be taken, the priority to be allocated to it and complete related tasks such as summarising a report or drafting a reply to an email. There is usually tight time constraint.

The exercise will probably start by describing the background scenario. Subject matter is usually related to the job you are applying for.

- Typically you will be given one to two hours to complete the tasks which will consist of a large number of items (perhaps 20 or more) to see how well you can handle several complex tasks in a short period.
- Some tasks may just require a simple yes or no answer. Other items may need a longer response, such as drafting a reply to a customer complaint, writing a report, delegating tasks to colleagues or recommending action to superiors. You may need to analyse information for some items (calculating budgets or sales figures, using information provided). *New items may be added while the exercise is in progress.*
- At the end you may be debriefed by a selector and asked to discuss the decisions you made and the reasons for these or you might be asked to prepare a memo outlining your priorities for action, or make a short presentation.
- In-tray exercises are usually done individually but can also be run as a group exercise.

Networking

Do not underestimate the importance of continually developing and nurturing your own list of key networks, both within your own organisation and beyond. This is simply the process of developing meaningful contacts so as to maximise your opportunities. The key is in ongoing development and nurturing. It is a two-way exercise, people-focused activity where you connect with others. Once you build a relationship, networking is following up and maintaining that contact over a long period of time.

Objectives of networking

- To present your skills and abilities to people who can help in your job search
- Continually provide a sharper focus on your career objectives
- To locate potential opportunities

Why networking will work for you

- Organisations depend on people to run and make key decisions, ultimate survival of any organisation is reliant upon this salient fact
- When you approach people, they will instinctively prefer to say 'yes' than 'no'
- Everyone enjoys praise or recognition for achievement or expertise
- Individuals like to give advice from a basis of knowledge. This is enjoyable for most people
- People respond best to a gradual approach

How should you network?

Network with as many individuals as you can. Start with your immediate colleagues, line management, senior managers, individuals in different departments etc. You need not limit

Coach's Tip

Keep a notebook of the favours people have done for you and write each one a short thank you note

your general networking to your organisation; don't forget your customers and external contacts as well as your partner's work colleagues, parents at your child's new school. Initiate conversations with others who are alone. Ask questions and become an active listener. Greet everyone with smile and a friendly hello followed by a positive comment or open-ended question to get a conversation going. At any party or other gathering, approach people standing alone and draw them into conversation. Most people hesitate to approach a group of friends already talking. The individual standing alone will welcome your approach, and you will find it easy to make your first networking contact.

When meeting new individuals, it is important to be able to clearly express who you are. Be prepared to say who you are and what you do in 25 words or less, in a way that will make the other person want to know more about you. Then, immediately ask questions to learn more about your new contact. In this 'elevator speech' you could start by very brief overview of your role and one or two notable achievements.

Developing networking process

During the course of your conversation, it is important to make people aware of what you are looking for, as well as how you could help them. Remember, networking is a two-way process. Others can't help you unless they know what you need. You will have greater success approaching networking as market research on your own behalf instead of asking "Do you have a job for me?" Focus on ways you can set up informational follow up meetings. These meetings will allow you to find out more information about your career field and your options, while gaining valuable insight from a professional on how to market yourself. Networking is a reciprocal process. It is about getting and giving information, resources, advice and referrals. Keep a mental 'give list' . . . a tip, idea, resource or recent discovery you can share. Your 'get list' will be information you are seeking, people you want to meet and referrals you would like to have.

Make sure you have business cards with your details that you can pass on after getting to know a person and a name badge that is easily readable if you are at a networking function. It is very important to follow up with people you have met, and that means having some kind of system in place so that you remember what you spoke about. Try jotting down a few notes on the back of business cards right after meeting someone. Ideally you should follow up within **48** hours. As time goes by, use every opportunity to send a follow-up personal note or e-mail, a thank you, congratulations or a relevant article of information.

Building up a new network requires time and effort. You may be able to springboard off of your "home" network for contacts in a new country, but often you have to start at square one. If you can think of networking not as a pressure, 'hard sell' situation but as a chance to learn more about the field you are hoping to pursue and to build relationships with new and interesting people, you will eventually make the right connections and find a job.

Final thoughts

The higher you rise up the corporate ladder, the more you will need to show your ability to communicate with people across business functions and at all levels. Think about ways that you can achieve this within the normal boundaries of your job, and then think beyond the boundaries of your role. What can you demonstrate that would be useful experience for the future? For example, looking after the sales team in your manager's absence and handling delegation well will allow you to develop your skills and get yourself noticed.

If your company invests in individual development, request a mentor. This will show that you are thinking about your future within the business, and that you are working on your skills and experience of tomorrow. It will also help boost confidence when it comes to communicating with more senior colleagues.

Find out as much as you can about the strategic direction of your department and company; it is much easier to align what you are doing if you are clear about higher level objectives and goals.

Many people are not good at taking compliments, but you need to be clear about, and proud of your achievements and do take well-deserved praise gracefully. Ask your manager 'that experience was useful to me, how would you build on that if you were me?' This should help your manager to get engaged in thinking about how to use your skills in the business, and often opens up new opportunities.

Not everyone can speak to their manager about ambitions, especially if the manager feels threatened by your plans. This is a judgement call. If you feel your manager will support your bid to take his role when he leaves, you should get some clear feedback on the areas you need to work on in order to be seen as a credible successor. Your manager may be able to do some ground work on your behalf and discreetly drop your name into conversation with the right individuals as plans are made to fill the vacancy.

Try to become more visible and take the opportunity to mix with individuals that matter, the key decision makers and share your success stories at the appropriate times. Ensure you get the balance right so that you are not seen as overplaying your achievements.

Part seven **Summary**

- It is important to enjoy your job and get satisfaction out of what you are doing.
- Successful career development starts by an effective internal assessment.
- Ask yourself what areas excite you and what would you enjoy doing in 2, 3 or 5 years from today?
- Sales and Marketing represent the bulk of career options open to you.
- Sales Management and Product/Brand Management are ideal career options which will build your skills and confidence.
- Sales Training role can be very satisfying particularly if you enjoy developing others and like the personal interactions in the field base sales teams.
- Use all the available self assessment careers tools which can help make your assessment of career options and directions more effective.
- Develop a high quality cv that represents you in the best way.
- Excellent performance in interviews is about self confidence. This confidence will come from good preparation, planning and knowledge leading up to the interview.
- View assessment centres as a good opportunity to showcase your capabilities. Approach them with positive energy, be relaxed and see the results.
- Do not underestimate the power of networking and do put the effort to make it work—it will pay dividends when you need it.

Part Eight | Individual factors

The difference between a successful person and others is not a lack of strength, not a lack of knowledge, but rather a lack in will
Vince Lombardi

What motivates you and how do you rise up to the constant challenges in your sales role? This chapter looks at personal factors that will help you progress and develop so that you have sustained energy and you can perform at your best.

As you progress with your career and you are busy exploring all the ways that will help you, it is worth reflecting on a few areas that will assist in demonstrating your capability and which can help you rise to the challenge. Figure 8.1 shows these four areas:

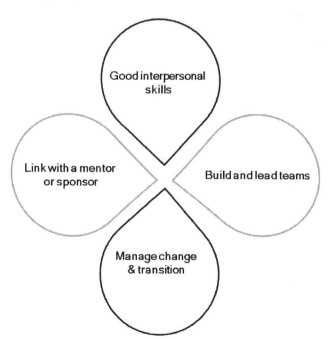

Figure 8.1 Key factors to focus upon

Good interpersonal skills

As you progress in your career, your ability to make relationships becomes more paramount. More senior roles will demand greater degree of political sensitivity because at that level, relationships go beyond everyday tasks and are focussed on the long term business viability. Some potential managers will attempt to display an over confident communication style that can come across very arrogant. There is no substitute for genuine self confidence, so it is important that you put time into your personal development to really know yourself well, understand your values, and create a clear picture of what you want. With this knowledge, good communication and an easy manner should be seen as natural.

Write good e-mails

This is an essential art. It is very easy to overlook the basics especially when you are in a hurry or have competing agendas. It is, however, important to adhere to basics of spelling, grammar and punctuation so that your message cannot be easily misinterpreted. The style of the message will of course depend on the recipient, but think through what you are writing and to whom so that your company's reputation is always enhanced and never compromised.

The following factors will be helpful:

- Emails should be a short form of communication. It should be brief and to the point.
- Avoid long passages especially to senior managers who will be busy, besides on a small screen it can be inconvenient for the recipient. If you need to go into more detail, send an attachment. If this is not possible

then consider breaking your message into small 'chunks' with a headline before each new section.

- Use a spell check to ensure you don't send obvious spelling mistakes.
- Text messaging speak has crept into emails. This is fine for your known subjects or where you need to be very concise but best avoided to external individuals.
- Use the right lower and upper case as messages written entirely in lower case letters can suggest something written in a hurry.
- Try to limit the use of acronyms and abbreviations, especially when one or more of the recipients may not understand otherwise explain what they mean
- Use the appropriate style to address the recipient: 'Hi', 'Hello' as informal and 'Dear' as more formal.
- Make it clear if your message is urgent so that recipients can prioritise with so much noise from daily in box entries. Use the relevant email facility to highlight importance but don't over use this. Avoid using too many capital letters to indicate urgency and importance. This may also be negatively interpreted as 'shouting'.
- Finally email styles differ from country to country and languages. If you have to email international contacts take a lead from their messages and mirror this style.

INFORMAL	MORE FORMAL	VERY FORMAL
Cheers	Best	Yours
Thanks	Best wishes	Yours
Thnx	All the best	Sincerely (if subject is known)
Ta	Best wishes	Faithfully (if subject is unknown)
All the best	Many thanks	
Later	Regards	
See you	Kind regards	

Figure 8.2: Rounding off emails

Managing your inbox

Keeping your inbox clean and tidy is an invaluable habit. It shows great organisation and will avoid missing important communications. Taking control of your inbox is really taking control of your work. Excess emails will slow down the system as well as clogging up your company's inbox facility.

If you are faced with large volumes of emails, you will need to prioritise your inbox. Try the following tactics:-

- Check names of senders: were you expecting and how quickly do you need to deal with them?
- Check the subject matter: is it urgent or just for your information? Does it concern you directly or should be forwarded to someone else?

- Check the priority given by senders: do they really mean urgent?
- Is it obvious spam and should be deleted?
- Check the timing of the message; has it been there a long time?

You can reply in stages with a brief acknowledgement and commitment with specific date as follow up. Taking a staged approach is useful as it will allow you to maintain contact whilst not interrupting other work that could be important.

Coach's Tip

Alternative to emails include instant messaging, voicemail and teleconferencing

Set a time when you can commit to handling your emails. If your emails are available on a mobile device you can deal with all urgent and quick emails during the day when you are out in the field reducing the workload later in the day.

Ensure you organise your email folders so that you can have swift access and retrieval later. Check your company policy for email retention.

Do use the 'out of office reply' facility so that your volume load after returning from holidays is minimised. State when you will return and that you will deal with the mail upon your return.

Build and lead teams

This is a key skill that distinguishes credible senior managers; the ability put together the right individuals and leads them to a defined goal. Success will come from communicating clear objectives as well as taking the time to understand the skills, motives and personal values of the team. Relationships should ideally be open with healthy flow of feedback so that everyone is aligned with the common purpose. Inserting milestones and KPIs will be helpful so that progress can be monitored and success shared.

Empowerment is important so that individuals can perform to the best of his or her abilities. Trust and understanding will help.

If teamwork is essential, decide which responsibilities can be assigned to the right individuals. Make individuals develop ownership. This will, of course, depend on your role and responsibility but as you start to take a more leading role, you should develop the confidence in being able to direct and shape the outcome through others.

Coach's Tip

Understand the tasks and be aware of the skills, experience and approach of the team

Manage change and transition

Changing market dynamics, economy, the healthcare sector etc will add pressure to the prevailing business and organisational model. The impact can either be immediate or delayed. Current pace of change means that effects are felt much sooner in the field than in days gone by. Linking with your company's strategic direction and proactively sensing the direction in the field are important and this knowledge and insight should be used to help direct you're own and other colleagues energy towards embracing and working with potential challenges. In short, remain flexible and actively look for ways of making things happen, keeping your colleagues motivated and continue to learn from new experiences—these are all characteristics of senior managers. Loyalty and solidarity do count when a company is going through significant change.

Link with a mentor or sponsor

No doubt you will have seen individuals who have been promoted on the basis of those who they know, not what they know, but this may not be the guarantee of long term success. What is much

Coach's Tip

If there is a senior manager that you get on well with, why not request him or her to be your mentor? This will be invaluable in giving you direction and advice.

better is to build a robust network of relationships that will support you solely due to your potential and personal integrity. You can be sure that you are not reliant on the perception by others (and over whom you have no control) but instead, you are judged on your own talent and attributes.

Go through your network list and identify those who can act as role models, potential coaches and mentors for different aspects of your development plan. You should frame your request in development terms stating that you feel you have a lot to offer and would appreciate their guidance.

Your ideal mentor or sponsor should be someone at least one or two levels above your current grade. That individual can help nudge your career in the right direction: hearing about possible openings, avoiding career traps and giving you access to decision makers.

Managing your image

How you come across and impact you make on others is important, yet many of us do not consciously think about this. Managing your image well will increase the confidence others have in you and will help support career opportunities for you.

Coach's Tip

To improve your chances of promotion, take an active interest in the business and understand the key issues...you need confident communication and an ability to build relationships

Have a look at figure 8.3 which illustrates the key aspects to think about in making the right impact.

First impressions are important and so it is important that the precious first few moments when you are meeting someone are orchestrated well.

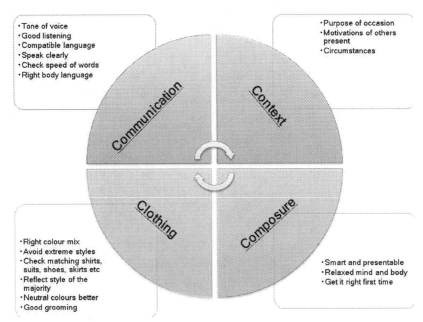

- Tone of voice
- Good listening
- Compatible language
- Speak clearly
- Check speed of words
- Right body language

Communication

Context

- Purpose of occasion
- Motivations of others present
- Circumstances

Clothing

Composure

- Right colour mix
- Avoid extreme styles
- Check matching shirts, suits, shoes, skirts etc
- Reflect style of the majority
- Neutral colours better
- Good grooming

- Smart and presentable
- Relaxed mind and body
- Get it right first time

Figure 8.3: Making the right impression

Image management is a subtle skill; avoid trying too hard. You can practice in front of a mirror or with a trusted colleague. You will need to engage actively in creating and maintaining the right impression.

Dress sense

Your appearance and wearing the appropriate attire will embed the right credibility within the internal as well as the external environment in which you work in.

An appealing image requires the right coordination of suits, colours, materials and patterns so that it reinforces your intended image message. The wrong or cheap colour, material and patterns will detract from a professional image.

The colours that you wear against the background of your facial colour are important so that you make the right impact on others and for holding attention to your face rather than your attire.

Generally dark cool colours (such as black, charcoal and navy) are seen as authoritarian and credible although jet black suits may come across as unfriendly in some countries. Colour contrast will help others to remember you:

- High contrast: bright, dark combinations is power dressing and can come across as intimidating
- Medium contrast: light, dark combinations are ideal and professionally effective
- Low contrast: little or no colour difference between garments, can represent 'low' presence and not effective in most business settings

Managing perceptions

Everyone has differing views of the work environment as each individual brings different cultural backgrounds, life experiences and personal values. This can affect your interaction with others. Your behaviour, skills, style and approach to others will further affect relationships. As you move to more senior roles, it becomes more important to be able to understand and manage perception of others. With a deal of thought, motivation and sense of self awareness this can be achieved easily. At the very least you should be aware of the impressions your behaviour creates.

Why is impression management important?

Careers are managed by individuals rather than organisations and often the impression that you have created for them will be the key to their decision making when it comes to career development. You are judged on not only what you do, but how you do it. People usually hold on to first impressions and this can be difficult to change. To make the change you need to first understand the both the existing perception and the one you wish to create. You will need an opportunity to create a bridge between the two and convey a different message. You must, however, be honest and sincere as otherwise this will be difficult to sustain in the long term.

Coach's Tip

Behavioural change is not as easy as learning a new skill - give yourself some time, and persevere

Perception strategy

Having an accurate understanding of your own skills and capabilities is important and this will require courage and commitment.

Start by gaining informal feedback from trusted peers and managers. Do remember that any feedback given will be a subjective point of view or an individual opinion. This should ideally be put into context with backed up examples whenever possible. Often 360 degree feedback surveys can be used, although these tend to focus on behaviour and competence. It is important to look for patterns in your behaviour, and reflect on when and why these may have occurred.

Focus on one aspect that you can change that will create a quick win. Try the following four actions:-

- **Communicate** your desired intentions to individuals who may be affected.
- **Gain support** from your colleagues or line manager to help keep you focussed. Good support group can be invaluable.
- **Find a coach** who can provide ongoing guidance. You will need impartial observations and someone who will encourage you to continue or change your strategy as you move forward.
- **Evaluate** your progress at each milestone in your plan, formally or informally. You should inform those who will be observing for feedback so they can consciously pay attention to your behaviour.

Finally, impression creation is through conscious activities and the awareness of your setting. You must define your target audience and align your values with theirs. Your communication style will require some adjustment and encourage feedback. Be aware of how you adjust and adapt your behaviour.

DO	DON'T
✓ Increase your awareness	✗ React emotionally to received feedback
✓ Be aware of effect of pressure on you and how others perceive this	✗ Become self centred
✓ Encourage feedback at appropriate pace	✗ Expect too much
✓ Allow others to have their choices	✗ Engage others in your own views of yourself
✓ Be aware of the impact you have on others	✗ Get defensive
✓ Interpret signals you send to others	✗ Become de-motivated
✓ Be visible at strategic moments	✗ Try too hard too quickly

Figure 8.4: Perception management

Writing good reports

Writing a well structured and well constructed report can be an invaluable skill especially as you progress in your career. Quite often, particularly in project work, individuals get overwhelmed by the scope and requirements and feel the need to include every little detail resulting in a very long document that is not fit for purpose.

Remember that the purpose of a written report is to present the relevant information upon which good decisions can be made or useful data can be reinterpreted for future use. Good reports have to be succinct, precise to the point and written very clearly. There must be logical flow of argument that can be followed easily.

Constructing a good report

The following aspects should be noted when you approach writing your report:

- **Have a clear aim and objective in mind.** It helps to visualise the final document in your mind. This should help you decide what to include and leave out.

- **Set the right context.** State the purpose and outcomes sought. You can set the expectations and guide the reader on how the contents of the report should be considered or applied.

Coach's Tip

Think hard about the reader in mind and try to address potential counter arguments in your report

- **Present the key issues.** State and address each issue separately and develop your argument logically. Be objective and avoid any personal opinions and commit to accurate data and findings or discussion points. Identify the themes that will be developed in the main body of the report and signpost any sections in which this will be done.

- **Understand the underlying issues.** Expand on the underlying causes and issues that emerge as a consequence. Explore any possible solutions; mention fully any implications including costs. This should assist the report into logical conclusion.

- **Appraise the future**. Put any possible future context into the report which will enhance it. This forward thinking can help you to explain why one decision is better than another.
- **Conclude and make recommendations**. Draw the report into logical conclusion and as a result of the preceding arguments your recommendations.

The following is a checklist that should help you:

Context	Are the purpose and the outcomes clear? Have you considered the reader in mind?
Organisation	Is the document logically ordered? Is there an obvious beginning, middle and end to your report? Is there a logical thread linking your report together?
Presentation	Layout, format, use of tables and illustrations etc. Ensure enough white space to make document inviting to the reader
Content	All key issues covered? Are assumptions outlines? Are the arguments clear and free from personal or unbiased views?
Style	Is the writing succinct and clear? Is the document laid out neatly? Have you checked for grammar and spelling?
Conclusions and recommendations	Are the recommendations and conclusions free of personal bias? Are they natural outcome from the report?

Managing your time well

The ability to manage all the various daily tasks including customer interactions, admin and internal communications is important. This requires ability to plan well and at the same time being able to focus on the present, which is an effective way to work through any laborious task. Whilst the availability of new mobile technology should be helping to reduce the daily complexity, it may actually add to the workload unless you have a disciplined approach to the daily use of such devices.

You should be aware of the daily choices you have to make and these will relate to your overall life balance and the values you hold.

Assess the tasks you are being asked to do and why. If any are outside your area of responsibility speak to your line manager and clarify the boundaries. You may have to be more realistic about your time management capability and work hard towards developing sound habits that are applied daily. Build in, whenever possible, some slack in the schedule to give yourself the best possible chance of meeting deadlines.

Conducting time audit

This is an assessment of the balance between the demands placed upon you by your work commitments and those commitments outside of work. Start by asking yourself if the way you presently manage your time is working well, and if so, what amendments could improve the quality of your life?

Whatever your current situation, it is important to bear a couple of points in mind:

- Do you have good awareness of the wider world which surrounds you and how the time components relate to each other? Here you can include the working practice of your company head office as well as styles and preferences of your customers and the market in general.

- Do you effectively prioritise? There simply is not enough time in a day to be able to complete everything possible so the need is to pick and choose according to importance.

Take a sheet of paper and write out all the key demands in your life and make an accurate forecast of the daily commitment that is required. Figure 8.5 gives an example of some of the areas to think about. Mark the number of hours that you need to dedicate to each key area in the day, month or year. This will give you a representation of what is required. Compare this to how you currently allocate your time commitment.

Coach's Tip

Look for patterns in the way you use time...check that your meetings are not always running late

Do you need to make any major changes to the way that you work? What are the areas that you need to concentrate upon which will enhance your output? Take a highlighter pen and mark areas that need attention. Think about activities that presently can be trimmed that is wasted time during the day. For example, if you work out regularly is there a club or gym closer reducing your travel time or can you change the time you go?

Daily activity	Required time (hrs)	Current time (hrs)	Difference
Daily work hours			
Travel time to customers			
Lunch and dinner			
Customer meetings			
Socialising			
Exercise			
Household duties			

Figure 8.5: Conducting time audit

If you feel you are overloaded with your role, do relook at the workload, prioritise and then refer back to the company's job description. Do speak with your manager and aim to work together on areas that add value to your role and career versus those that can be discarded or delegated to someone else.

Coach's Tip

Lead a balance between procrastinating on key decisions, being stressed out workaholic and being too relaxed

Finally planning is absolutely essential. Bring time management as a conscious exercise and this will build awareness and awareness is the key step into action.

DO	DON'T
Carry out a 'time audit'	Spend time on unnecessary activities
Be realistic about how long activities take	Cram in too many activities
Build in time for yourself	Blame others for your own disorganisation
Anticipate pressures of commitments	Make commitments that you cannot meet
Proactively communicate with others where there are time conflicts	Expect others to make up for what you cannot do
Plan ahead	Give up
Build in time for learning and reflection	Try to take the impossible

8.6: Some dos and don'ts of time management

Coping with stress

Managing your customers well, dealing with internal colleagues, driving to meet customers, handling meetings, short deadlines, sending approvals and managing meetings . . . just some of the daily tasks that will be expected from you. There will be occasions when there is additional pressure in your work, particularly around times when you are behind budget or have recently launched a new product or have to manage complex set of meetings. It is at these times that you will feel additional pressure. The problem is that the stress that emanates from these and other events can make us do or say things, that after reflection, we wish we had not.

When do you know you are stressed?

Pressure can be stimulating and motivating but when this exceeds our ability to cope, stress is the result. Such stress cannot be sustained for too long because it can lead to illness, depression etc. Do focus on your wellbeing, any signs; either behavioural or physical symptoms mentioned below can indicate excessive stress. Have a look at the list below and if you notice any behavioural symptoms with the associated physical symptoms, do seek professional help and support at the earliest convenience.

Behavioural symptoms	Physical symptoms
• Suppressed anger	• Lack of appetite
• Difficulty in concentrating	• Nervous twitch or nail biting
• Constant tiredness	• Cramps or muscle spasms
• Irritable with colleagues or customers	• Nausea
• Decision making difficulties	• Fainting spells
• Feeling out of control	• Insomnia
• Poor or disrupted sleep	• Indigestion or heart burn

Daily work challenges

Make a note of the potential and actual pressures at work. The list below gives an indication of the regularly occurring possible stress triggers. We sincerely hoped that you do not have to address any significant stressful event such as redundancy, bullying from management or colleagues or coping with a dysfunctional corporate culture (either excessive working hours or autocratic management style). The following is a list of daily challenges, may be you can think of others.

Personality differences with colleague	Travelling to meet customers
Red tape and excessive paperwork	Too much responsibility
Travelling to meet customers	Unsupportive partner
Unclear goals from manager	Health concerns
Too many meetings	No clear career direction
Conflicting appointments	Tight deadlines
Family problems	Faulty IT equipment
Competitor activities	Worried about job security

Knowing the causes of pressure

There are many causes of stress and pressure many of which will be linked. Some of the most obvious are:

- Time pressure, too much to do and too little time to do it in
- Insufficient resources: not enough budget or manpower available
- Unreasonable demands, especially from line management
- Insufficient training
- Promising to do too much too quickly
- Lack of job security

Taking control of stress

It is often at stressful occasions when we are tested to our limits that we realise our limitations and capabilities. The key point is to regain control so that you can alleviate the short term stress and address long term issues in a measured and thoughtful manner. Try the following:-

- Whenever possible anticipate where pressure will come from
- Tasks which you find challenging should be broken down into smaller manageable chunks
- Plan routine tasks with the most enjoyable
- Communicate proactively with other stakeholders particularly when working on projects so that expectations especially time deadlines can be managed easily. Learn to say 'I don't know' or 'I don't understand' a task or objective, this will release some pressure
- Reserve your prime time in the day, when you have the highest energy levels for complex or demanding tasks
- Manage technology effectively: answer phone calls appropriately, prioritise emails according to importance to your objectives and try to switch off the mobile phone when you need to concentrate on your key tasks, as any interruptions can be derailing

Learn to relax and take the rest that your body and mind require. During a stressful day this may mean taking 15 minute to half an hour where possible to eat well and focus the mind away from work, such as listening to iPod, reading a book or newspaper etc.

If the project that you are managing is stressful, focus on the decisions that are taken at early stages so that the right focus, direction and tone is set. Creative solutions and thinking can be helpful.

Achieving the right balance

Leading a healthy lifestyle is absolutely essential to coping with all the demands of your job as well as your personal and family commitments. This should at the very least help to ensure that you maintain the right energy for optimal performance at all times. The two key components are diet and exercise.

Diet

A healthy balanced diet is essential. Getting the balance is the key. There may be days when you 'over do it' but this should be the exception rather than the rule. Simply eating too many unnecessary calories will slow the body right down and this can make you sluggish and in the long run unproductive. You should aim for a good size breakfast with light lunch and an evening meal that is not too late. You will need to adjust your routine when attending meetings and conferences but again common sense is important especially when it comes to alcohol consumption. Try to avoid missing lunch or other meals because you are 'too busy'. Your body is very capable of adapting to your routine and if this routine is heavy meals late at night to compensate for missing lunch, this is not good in the long run. Also being on the road does not mean that fast food is always the preferred option, simply plan your lunch needs into your schedule as you are travelling so that you either arrive at an appropriate venue or have a prepared lunch with you and stop for lunch. Make sure you keep hydrated preferably with plain water depending on your climate.

Your overall diet pattern should contain a combination as follows:

- **Complex Carbohydrates** are foods that will help release energy slowly during the long hours of fasting.

Complex carbohydrates are found in grains and seeds, like barley, wheat, oats, millet, semolina, beans, lentils, wholemeal flour, whole grain rice, etc

- **Fibre-rich foods** are also digested slowly and include bran, cereals, whole wheat, grains and seeds, potatoes with the skin, vegetables such as green beans and almost all fruit including apricots, prunes, figs, etc
- **Foods to avoid** are the heavily-processed, fast-burning foods that contain refined carbohydrates in the form of sugar, white flour, etc. as well as of course, too much fatty foods (e.g. cakes, biscuits, chocolates and sweets, fast food outlets)

If you are currently eating an unhealthy diet, firstly commit to change but your taste buds will need some time to make the adjustment. Then make the change gradually. Substituting a piece of fruit for a high sugar chocolate bar for example makes good sense. Try making regular juices containing fruit and vegetables

Exercise

Any form of exercise that you engage in should be enjoyable so that you have the motivation to sustain it over a long period of time. Try to focus on exercise as play time that has an element of fun. Try to achieve the right balance of exercise that will give you good workout according to your needs and that you can continue to build up and reach new goals in. High energy demanding sports such as squash will provide good cardiovascular workload and gym based strength training will give the muscular endurance to cope with everyday challenges. Team sports like soccer are also great way of socialising and staying fit. The key point is that whatever activity you engage in should be maintained regularly and consistently to provide value.

Time to move on

As we have discussed the sales representative role is highly fulfilling, satisfying and exhilarating. By excelling in this role you will have learned so much about your own capabilities managing your own territory, customers, internal colleagues etc. The skills and the knowledge that you have acquired is an ideal launch for further career options we have explored in part seven. For many sales representatives, the thrill of the role, challenges in the field, customer relationships and meetings all mean they are very satisfied and would not even think about changing the status quo. For them satisfaction comes from their sales achievements, new product launches, overcoming barriers to change by their customers and being part of active team.

For others there comes a moment when change is inevitable. Impulsion towards career progression as well as the desire to learn new skills and added responsibility will drive the search for promotion or change in direction. So when is the best moment for this to happen? There are, of course, no hard and fast rules governing timing of career progression, your own circumstances, opportunities in your chosen department or company as well as growth in the market will all be important. Additionally, look out for the following signs:

- Unsolicited affirmations from colleagues—clear that you are excelling in your role and your output is recognised by your peers
- Frequent requests or your advice sought—recognition of your capabilities that might be specific to one or two areas or general covering a range of activities

- Seems all too easy—you are on top of your territory as well as effectively managing all expectation and the challenges that you face

You should ideally spend 18-24 months in a sales role to derive the maximum experience and exposure. Your career dialogue and intentions should be part of the ongoing effort with your manager so that you can both manage the whole process effectively. Having the clear vision, direction and understanding is the right basis to pursue promotion.

Making the difference

Your success and longevity will be a confluence of many factors. As we have seen many factors will be within your own area of control and only you can make the critical input and difference. Striking the right balance will enable you to reach your aspirations in the right manner and according to your time schedule. Of all the factors in figure 8.7, the *tenacity and concern for achievement* are two factors that can distinguish you as a star performer from an average one. These can only come from within and it is your responsibility to objectively consider whether you need to focus and work on these factors. This may not be easy when events and circumstances are challenging but you do need to take a long term view.

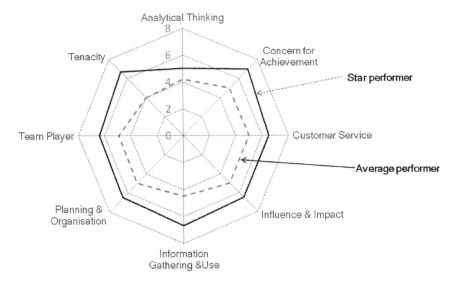

Figure 8.7: Distinguishing performance factors

Do the basics right, focus on outcomes; be clear on your strategic objectives and priorities; keep a positive winning attitude.

This book, any book, cannot pretend to give the universal solutions to all challenges in your role. If used wisely, it can help accelerate your learning from experience and hence your journey to success.

Enjoy the journey.

GOOD LUCK!

Part eight Summary

- Focus on the key areas that will support your personal development: interpersonal skills, link with a mentor or sponsor, build and lead teams and manage transition and change.

- Good communications should be integral part of your interpersonal skills. As email communication will be a significant part of your daily communications, focus on getting the right quality and frequency. Ensure all your messages are clear and unambiguous.
- If you have the opportunity, take full advantage of building or leading a team. This will develop your confidence for future roles.
- Do consider the advantages of having a mentor or sponsor who can act as a guide and support your career development.
- Managing your image is about the way you control how others view you and the perception that will be made about you, so it is important that you pay attention to setting the right impression and style of dress etc.
- Write well structured reports, read carefully before any submission and pay attention to details that you may be asked about.
- Do reflect and understand any underlying causes of stress—think through the daily challenges and any links to stress. Seek help and support at your earliest opportunity, don't wait until the issue or problem becomes difficult to manage, far better to talk through with someone.
- 'Look after your body and your body will look after you'. Develop good eating and exercise habits and integrate these into your daily routine.
- Continually develop the tenacity and concern for achievements as key attributes that will serve you well in the long term.

APPENDICES

Appendix 1: assessing career management direction

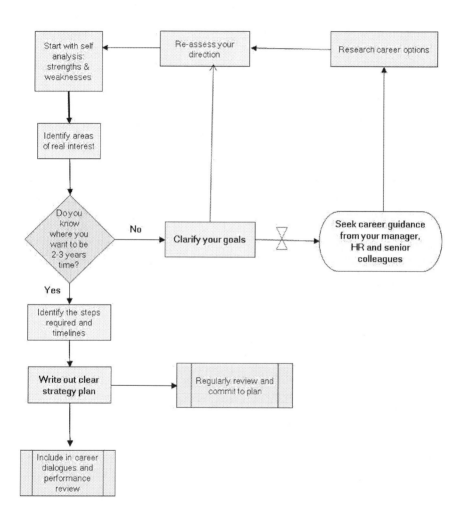

Appendix 2: CV and cover letters

Lina McEdwards
4499 Kingston Lane
Vancouver, BC 2992
(405) 887 9988
Lena.Mcedwards35@aol.com

This CV illustrates less than 5 years experience

Professional objective and profile

High calibre Pharmaceutical sales representative with experience building and leading sales operations and increasing revenue. Consistently successful in building and expanding territory with proven track record of surpassing market share goal. Customer service oriented with capability to successfully network with leading market decision makers and all levels of management.

Desire a sales management position which will provide a challenging opportunity to significantly contribute to efficiency, organisation, growth and profitability.

Education

Bachelor in Pharmacy Bpharm
Minor: Management and psychology
BRITISH COLUMBIA STATE UNIVERSITY
Vancouver, BC, 2004

Summary of accomplishments

Track record of success

Successful career goal accomplishments as a Territory Manager for Bannon Labs, Inc. steadily advanced to senior sales specialist.

Sales record

Ranked #1 for two key products in 2009 exemplifying strong presentation, negotiation and closing skills. Supporting Marketing Director in developing marketing strategies and marketing campaigns

Account Management

Proven track record in creating and maintaining new accounts for specialty care products

Leadership

Strong written and oral communications with ability to inspire colleagues to achieve team objectives

---

Professional Experience

Territory Sales Manager

BANNON LABS Inc., Vancouver, BC

2007 to present

Territory management: responsible for managing overall sales territory development throughout BC area including retail pharmacies, GPs, hospitals and wholesalers

Market share increase: in just 5 months, have surpassed 2010 company goal of 23.6% market share for *Trasic* to 29.9%. Increased market share for *Basuit* by 8% in 12 months surpassing market growth of 5%

Account Management: established growth plans for individual accounts and personally managed the implementation, coordination and execution through individual and group presentations and contract negotiations with Commercial colleague

Marketing: support team in designing campaign materials. Currently designing a marketing plan to sell pill cutters in conjunction with Basuit campaign for dialysis patients

Customer management: providing superior service by promptly responding to requests, inquiries and suggestions

Clear indication of accomplishments

Assistant Manager

Baskin Robbins, Vancouver,

2004-2007

Management: started as customer service rep and was quickly promoted to Assistant Manager. Assisted in managing overall operations and administration of the store

Personnel: assisted in interviewing and hiring employees. Delegated responsibilities and monitored overall job performances to ensure accuracy and adherence to company rules and regulations

Employee relations: encouraged and supported a team like work environment, which increased company morale, productivity and efficiency. Served as communications liaison between employees and upper management

Customer service: provided excellent service to customers which ensured customer satisfaction, repeat business and referrals

Inventory: assisted in monitoring inventory levels of food and beverages

Lina McEdwards
4499 Kingston Lane
Vancouver, BC 2992
(405) 887 9988
Lena.McEdwards35@aol.com

Date
Jeremy Caldwell
Sales Director
Fisher Pharmaceuticals Inc
2984 Hillsboro Avenue
Kansas City, Kansas 29993
Dear Mr Caldwell:

I am a highly motivated; goal oriented Pharmaceutical Sales Representative with an exemplary track record of achievement. I am now ready and confident of excelling in the **Regional Sales Management** role with Fisher. I have attached my CV so you may review my credentials in detail.

In addition to a Bachelor of Pharmacy degree from British Columbia State, I have more than 3 years experience as a Territory Manager for Bannon Labs Inc. My qualifications and experience includes:

- Excellent territory management skills increasing revenue year on year
- Solid organisational, management, interpersonal and communications skills with a proven track record of making sound decisions
- Strong troubleshooting skills with ability to research and identify problems and implement creative problem solving solutions

- Style which exhibits maturity, high energy, teamwork and the ability to relate to a wide variety of professionals
- Demonstrated leadership, communication and negotiating skills
- Proven ability to define issues, propose solutions and implement changes

Specific attributes are bulleted to draw the eye to this data

- Computer literate with knowledge and experience in all MS applications

I sincerely believe that, with my experience and career goals, I would be an asset to your organisation. I would like to request a personal interview at your earliest convenience so that we can discuss ways that I can significantly contribute to your company's goals. I am available to relocate if required.

Thank you for your time and consideration. I look forward to speaking with you soon.

Always be assertive about taking the next step

Sincerely,
Lena

Lena McEdwards
4499 Kingston Lane
Vancouver, BC 2992
(405) 887 9988
Lena.McEdwards35@aol.com

Date
Jeremy Caldwell
Sales Director
Fisher Pharmaceuticals Inc
2984 Hillsboro Avenue
Kansas City, Kansas 29993

> **This thank you letter re-emphasises qualities that would be beneficial to the company**

Dear Mr Caldwell:
I appreciate the time you gave me yesterday afternoon. I thoroughly enjoyed meeting you and discussing employment opportunities. I felt our meeting was both enjoyable and informative.

After thinking about your Regional Sales Management position and the goals you have set, I am confident that I will be able to exceed your expectations. I will build upon my experience and knowledge particularly of the Vancouver area and significant value. My record has been stellar, with numerous awards and bonuses for outstanding increase in revenues and new accounts.

I consider your Regional Sales Manager position to be consistent with my career goals. Additionally, your company is a leader in the industry, with an outstanding reputation for rewarding top performers, and I believe this job will be an excellent career move for me.

Look forward to hearing from you.

Sincerely,
Lena McEdwards

Nancy LeBlanc
Apartment 2B, 98 Airport Rd,
Bercy, Paris, 20865 France
(33) 367 2298
nancy.leblanc20@gmail.fr

Career Profile

Dynamic, profit and results oriented Medical Sales Specialist with over 7 years experience in leading sales teams for major pharmaceutical companies. Proven track record in sequential growth in market share and sales target achievements. Excellent analytical, planning, organisational and negotiation skills. Strong client relationships.

Desire a challenging opportunity in Product Management to contribute to growth and profitability

Summary of Sales Awards

- Presidents' Club, La Geneve, sales award, 2010
- Sales Leader, La Geneve, sales award 2009
- Representative of the Quarter, La Geneve, 2008, 2007
- Cardiovascular Alliance Teamwork Award, La Geneve 2009
- Circle of Merit award, Astral, 2006, 2005
- Customer mapping award, Astral, 2006
- Highest Market share award, Azure, 2004

Medical sales Experience

Angioplasty Sales Specialist
La Geneve Pharma Inc, Paris 2007 to present

Sales: initiated high volume sales programme and responsible for expanding business by penetrating key medical device throughout the country

Accomplishments: increased revenue from **$345k to $1.2m in 2.5 years**. This was the fastest revenue growth in the whole Region. Sold the largest single order worth $250k to American Hospital in Al Shifa's entire history. Recipient of two highest company sales awards: *Presidents' Club and Sales Leader*

Business Development: Established business plans for 5 new accounts that contributed to additional **40% growth** in sales; personally managed account calls, presentations and contract negotiations

Physician Education Training: planned, coordinated national and international meetings on coronary angioplasty/stent procedures

Marketing: worked with Marketing Director to conceptualise and design innovative marketing and sales materials for use by sales teams

Medical Sales Representative
Astral Pharmaceuticals
Provence and Cote de Azure Region, 2005-2007

Sales: Led sales cycle from initial client consultation through presentations, price negotiations and closings. Solicited and gained new clients as well as maintaining existing accounts

Business Development: Hired to reposition and grow market share in the territory. Expanded market penetration by 20% and provided direction for long term business focus to meet company goals

Sales accomplishments: won Circle of Merit award, two years 2005 and 2006 as well as the Customer Mapping award 2006. Improved market share from lowest ranking of 9th to 2nd. Expanded market penetration of **Lozite** by 90% during period of budgetary constraints

Systems development: created, developed and incorporated a new system to record sales call information, which increased team efficiency

Market Research: Coordinated market research activities and surveys.

Cardiovascular Sales Representative
Azure Pharmaceuticals, Provence, 2003-2005

Sales accomplishments: Responsible for selling pharmaceutical brands to physicians and hospitals. Built market share from 14% to 28% for **Bisol** in one year. Achieved #2 market share for ANSAID, in the highly competitive market of non steroidals. Won highest market share award 2004.

Education

Bachelor of Science (BS) in Biology with Management studies *(majored in Marketing)*
ST NICHOLAS UNIVERSITY, Marseille, France

Dear Mr James,

I was speaking with your colleague Edward Reed recently and he suggested I should contact you. Ed tells me you have considerable expertise in e-learning and digital marketing and would be able to provide me with helpful advice.

I would like to utilise my customer relationships by adding new and innovative ways to deliver our core messages and enhance physician learning.

This is also in line with my overall broad objective of a Marketing career. Please understand that I am not expecting you to know of possible positions that may arise. I am just seeking to improve my understanding and would welcome the opportunity to hear how things work, or not, from your perspective.

I would be most grateful if we could meet for about twenty minutes or so to discuss these issues and will telephone you shortly to arrange a convenient date.

Many thanks.

Kind Regards
Amy Stuart

INDEX

Usage restrictions   49

V

venue   19, 71, 74, 142

W

well constructed report   132
well organised   12, 41, 77
working relationship   28, 38-42,
   45, 55

workload   64, 125, 135, 137, 143
Write good e-mails   122
Writing good reports   132

Y

year end annual performance
   appraisal   71